The Taming of the Shrew

By Edward de Vere

Art:
Portrait of Edward de Vere
17th Earl of Oxford (1550-1604)

This edition produced by
Verus Publishing

V | P

www.verusbooks.com

ISBN: 978-1-951267-38-4
Imprint / Publisher: Verus Publishing

The Author

Edward de Vere, 17th Earl of Oxford

Biography and Bibliography
After the Play

A Preverse

Drone on ye learned scholars of the day
As to with whom the words ahead the credit lay.
For our part though can be no further doubt
That the author of these words has been found out
To be a person lordly and refined
On whom the light of wit so boldly shined
That to keep this wit from tearing in the fray
He gave another, lesser wit his say.

Now let the least of wits
That writes these paltry lines
Yield to him whose peerless name
Should be with reverence spake.
Let this name be not of history's misassigns
Whose pen and verse have made the earth to shake.

The Taming of the Shrew

By Edward de Vere

The Main Characters

Katherina (Kate) Minola – The "Shrew"

Bianca Minola – Sister of Katherina

Baptista Minola – Father of Katherina and Bianca

Petruchio – Suitor to Katherina

Gremio – Elderly suitor to Bianca

Lucentio – Suitor to Bianca

Hortensio – Suitor to Bianca and Petruchio's friend

Grumio – Petruchio's manservant

Tranio – Lucentio's manservant

Biondello – A servant of Lucentio

Vincentio – The father of Lucentio

Widow – Wooed by Hortensio

Pedant – Pretends to be Vincentio

Haberdasher

Tailor

Curtis, Nathaniel, Joseph, Peter, Nicholas and Philip-
                    – All servants of Petruchio
An Officer

———

Characters appearing in the Induction:

Christopher Sly – A drunken tinker
Hostess - Proprietress of an alehouse
Lord – Plays a prank on Sly
Bartholomew – The Lord's page boy
The Lord's Huntsman
Players, Servingmen & A Messenger

And now, the Play...

INDUCTION

SCENE I.

Before an alehouse on a heath.

Enter Hostess and SLY

SLY

I'll pheeze you, in faith.

Hostess

A pair of stocks, you rogue!

SLY

Ye are a baggage: the Slys are no rogues; look in
the chronicles; we came in with Richard Conqueror.
Therefore paucas pallabris; let the world slide: sessa!

Hostess

You will not pay for the glasses you have burst?

SLY

No, not a denier. Go by, Jeronimy: go to thy cold
bed, and warm thee.

Hostess

I know my remedy; I must go fetch the
third--borough.

Exit

SLY

Third, or fourth, or fifth borough, I'll answer him
by law: I'll not budge an inch, boy: let him come,
and kindly.

Falls asleep

Horns winded. Enter a Lord from hunting, with his train

Lord

Huntsman, I charge thee, tender well my hounds:
Brach Merriman, the poor cur is emboss'd;
And couple Clowder with the deep--mouth'd brach.
Saw'st thou not, boy, how Silver made it good
At the hedge-corner, in the coldest fault?
I would not lose the dog for twenty pound.

First Huntsman

Why, Belman is as good as he, my lord;
He cried upon it at the merest loss
And twice to-day pick'd out the dullest scent:
Trust me, I take him for the better dog.

Lord

Thou art a fool: if Echo were as fleet,
I would esteem him worth a dozen such.
But sup them well and look unto them all:
To-morrow I intend to hunt again.

First Huntsman

I will, my lord.

Lord

What's here? one dead, or drunk? See, doth he breathe?

Second Huntsman

He breathes, my lord. Were he not warm'd with ale,
This were a bed but cold to sleep so soundly.

Lord

O monstrous beast! how like a swine he lies!
Grim death, how foul and loathsome is thine image!
Sirs, I will practise on this drunken man.
What think you, if he were convey'd to bed,
Wrapp'd in sweet clothes, rings put upon his fingers,
A most delicious banquet by his bed,
And brave attendants near him when he wakes,
Would not the beggar then forget himself?

First Huntsman

Believe me, lord, I think he cannot choose.
Second Huntsman
It would seem strange unto him when he waked.
Lord
Even as a flattering dream or worthless fancy.
Then take him up and manage well the jest:
Carry him gently to my fairest chamber
And hang it round with all my wanton pictures:
Balm his foul head in warm distilled waters
And burn sweet wood to make the lodging sweet:
Procure me music ready when he wakes,
To make a dulcet and a heavenly sound;
And if he chance to speak, be ready straight
And with a low submissive reverence
Say 'What is it your honour will command?'
Let one attend him with a silver basin
Full of rose-water and bestrew'd with flowers,
Another bear the ewer, the third a diaper,
And say 'Will't please your lordship cool your hands?'
Some one be ready with a costly suit
And ask him what apparel he will wear;
Another tell him of his hounds and horse,
And that his lady mourns at his disease:
Persuade him that he hath been lunatic;
And when he says he is, say that he dreams,
For he is nothing but a mighty lord.
This do and do it kindly, gentle sirs:
It will be pastime passing excellent,
If it be husbanded with modesty.
First Huntsman
My lord, I warrant you we will play our part,
As he shall think by our true diligence
He is no less than what we say he is.
Lord

The Taming of the Shrew — Induction

Take him up gently and to bed with him;
And each one to his office when he wakes.

Some bear out SLY. A trumpet sounds

Sirrah, go see what trumpet 'tis that sounds:

Exit Servingman

Belike, some noble gentleman that means,
Travelling some journey, to repose him here.

Re-enter Servingman

How now! who is it?
Servant
    An't please your honour, players
    That offer service to your lordship.
Lord
    Bid them come near.

Enter Players

Now, fellows, you are welcome.
Players
    We thank your honour.
Lord
    Do you intend to stay with me tonight?
A Player
    So please your lordship to accept our duty.
Lord
    With all my heart. This fellow I remember,
    Since once he play'd a farmer's eldest son:
    'Twas where you woo'd the gentlewoman so well:
    I have forgot your name; but, sure, that part
    Was aptly fitted and naturally perform'd.
A Player

9

I think 'twas Soto that your honour means.

Lord

    'Tis very true: thou didst it excellent.
    Well, you are come to me in a happy time;
    The rather for I have some sport in hand
    Wherein your cunning can assist me much.
    There is a lord will hear you play to-night:
    But I am doubtful of your modesties;
    Lest over-eyeing of his odd behavior,--
    For yet his honour never heard a play--
    You break into some merry passion
    And so offend him; for I tell you, sirs,
    If you should smile he grows impatient.

A Player

    Fear not, my lord: we can contain ourselves,
    Were he the veriest antic in the world.

Lord

    Go, sirrah, take them to the buttery,
    And give them friendly welcome every one:
    Let them want nothing that my house affords.

Exit one with the Players

    Sirrah, go you to Barthol'mew my page,
    And see him dress'd in all suits like a lady:
    That done, conduct him to the drunkard's chamber;
    And call him 'madam,' do him obeisance.
    Tell him from me, as he will win my love,
    He bear himself with honourable action,
    Such as he hath observed in noble ladies
    Unto their lords, by them accomplished:
    Such duty to the drunkard let him do
    With soft low tongue and lowly courtesy,
    And say 'What is't your honour will command,
    Wherein your lady and your humble wife

May show her duty and make known her love?'
And then with kind embracements, tempting kisses,
And with declining head into his bosom,
Bid him shed tears, as being overjoy'd
To see her noble lord restored to health,
Who for this seven years hath esteem'd him
No better than a poor and loathsome beggar:
And if the boy have not a woman's gift
To rain a shower of commanded tears,
An onion will do well for such a shift,
Which in a napkin being close convey'd
Shall in despite enforce a watery eye.
See this dispatch'd with all the haste thou canst:
Anon I'll give thee more instructions.

Exit a Servingman

I know the boy will well usurp the grace,
Voice, gait and action of a gentlewoman:
I long to hear him call the drunkard husband,
And how my men will stay themselves from laughter
When they do homage to this simple peasant.
I'll in to counsel them; haply my presence
May well abate the over-merry spleen
Which otherwise would grow into extremes.

Exeunt

SCENE II.

A bedchamber in the Lord's house.

*Enter aloft SLY, with Attendants; some with apparel, others
with basin and ewer and appurtenances; and Lord*

SLY
    For God's sake, a pot of small ale.

First Servant
    Will't please your lordship drink a cup of sack?
Second Servant
    Will't please your honour taste of these conserves?
Third Servant
    What raiment will your honour wear to-day?
SLY
    I am Christophero Sly; call not me 'honour' nor
    'lordship:' I ne'er drank sack in my life; and if
    you give me any conserves, give me conserves of
    beef: ne'er ask me what raiment I'll wear; for I
    have no more doublets than backs, no more stockings
    than legs, nor no more shoes than feet; nay,
    sometimes more feet than shoes, or such shoes as my
    toes look through the over-leather.
Lord
    Heaven cease this idle humour in your honour!
    O, that a mighty man of such descent,
    Of such possessions and so high esteem,
    Should be infused with so foul a spirit!
SLY
    What, would you make me mad? Am not I Christopher
    Sly, old Sly's son of Burtonheath, by birth a
    pedlar, by education a cardmaker, by transmutation a
    bear-herd, and now by present profession a tinker?
    Ask Marian Hacket, the fat ale-wife of Wincot, if
    she know me not: if she say I am not fourteen pence
    on the score for sheer ale, score me up for the
    lyingest knave in Christendom. What! I am not
    bestraught: here's--
Third Servant
    O, this it is that makes your lady mourn!
Second Servant
    O, this is it that makes your servants droop!

Lord

> Hence comes it that your kindred shuns your house,
> As beaten hence by your strange lunacy.
> O noble lord, bethink thee of thy birth,
> Call home thy ancient thoughts from banishment
> And banish hence these abject lowly dreams.
> Look how thy servants do attend on thee,
> Each in his office ready at thy beck.
> Wilt thou have music? hark! Apollo plays,

Music

> And twenty caged nightingales do sing:
> Or wilt thou sleep? we'll have thee to a couch
> Softer and sweeter than the lustful bed
> On purpose trimm'd up for Semiramis.
> Say thou wilt walk; we will bestrew the ground:
> Or wilt thou ride? thy horses shall be trapp'd,
> Their harness studded all with gold and pearl.
> Dost thou love hawking? thou hast hawks will soar
> Above the morning lark or wilt thou hunt?
> Thy hounds shall make the welkin answer them
> And fetch shrill echoes from the hollow earth.

First Servant

> Say thou wilt course; thy greyhounds are as swift
> As breathed stags, ay, fleeter than the roe.

Second Servant

> Dost thou love pictures? we will fetch thee straight
> Adonis painted by a running brook,
> And Cytherea all in sedges hid,
> Which seem to move and wanton with her breath,
> Even as the waving sedges play with wind.

Lord

> We'll show thee Io as she was a maid,
> And how she was beguiled and surprised,

As lively painted as the deed was done.
Third Servant
　　Or Daphne roaming through a thorny wood,
　　Scratching her legs that one shall swear she bleeds,
　　And at that sight shall sad Apollo weep,
　　So workmanly the blood and tears are drawn.
Lord
　　Thou art a lord, and nothing but a lord:
　　Thou hast a lady far more beautiful
　　Than any woman in this waning age.
First Servant
　　And till the tears that she hath shed for thee
　　Like envious floods o'er-run her lovely face,
　　She was the fairest creature in the world;
　　And yet she is inferior to none.
SLY
　　Am I a lord? and have I such a lady?
　　Or do I dream? or have I dream'd till now?
　　I do not sleep: I see, I hear, I speak;
　　I smell sweet savours and I feel soft things:
　　Upon my life, I am a lord indeed
　　And not a tinker nor Christophero Sly.
　　Well, bring our lady hither to our sight;
　　And once again, a pot o' the smallest ale.
Second Servant
　　Will't please your mightiness to wash your hands?
　　O, how we joy to see your wit restored!
　　O, that once more you knew but what you are!
　　These fifteen years you have been in a dream;
　　Or when you waked, so waked as if you slept.
SLY
　　These fifteen years! by my fay, a goodly nap.
　　But did I never speak of all that time?
First Servant

O, yes, my lord, but very idle words:
For though you lay here in this goodly chamber,
Yet would you say ye were beaten out of door;
And rail upon the hostess of the house;
And say you would present her at the leet,
Because she brought stone jugs and no seal'd quarts:
Sometimes you would call out for Cicely Hacket.

SLY

Ay, the woman's maid of the house.

Third Servant

Why, sir, you know no house nor no such maid,
Nor no such men as you have reckon'd up,
As Stephen Sly and did John Naps of Greece
And Peter Turph and Henry Pimpernell
And twenty more such names and men as these
Which never were nor no man ever saw.

SLY

Now Lord be thanked for my good amends!

ALL

Amen.

SLY

I thank thee: thou shalt not lose by it.

Enter the Page as a lady, with attendants

Page

How fares my noble lord?

SLY

Marry, I fare well for here is cheer enough.
Where is my wife?

Page

Here, noble lord: what is thy will with her?

SLY

Are you my wife and will not call me husband?
My men should call me 'lord:' I am your goodman.

15

Page
  My husband and my lord, my lord and husband;
  I am your wife in all obedience.
SLY
  I know it well. What must I call her?
Lord
  Madam.
SLY
  Al'ce madam, or Joan madam?
Lord
  'Madam,' and nothing else: so lords
  call ladies.
SLY
  Madam wife, they say that I have dream'd
  And slept above some fifteen year or more.
Page
  Ay, and the time seems thirty unto me,
  Being all this time abandon'd from your bed.
SLY
  'Tis much. Servants, leave me and her alone.
  Madam, undress you and come now to bed.
Page
  Thrice noble lord, let me entreat of you
  To pardon me yet for a night or two,
  Or, if not so, until the sun be set:
  For your physicians have expressly charged,
  In peril to incur your former malady,
  That I should yet absent me from your bed:
  I hope this reason stands for my excuse.
SLY
  Ay, it stands so that I may hardly
  tarry so long. But I would be loath to fall into
  my dreams again: I will therefore tarry in
  despite of the flesh and the blood.

The Taming of the Shrew – Induction

Enter a Messenger

Messenger
    Your honour's players, heating your amendment,
    Are come to play a pleasant comedy;
    For so your doctors hold it very meet,
    Seeing too much sadness hath congeal'd your blood,
    And melancholy is the nurse of frenzy:
    Therefore they thought it good you hear a play
    And frame your mind to mirth and merriment,
    Which bars a thousand harms and lengthens life.
SLY
    Marry, I will, let them play it. Is not a
    comondy a Christmas gambold or a tumbling-trick?
Page
    No, my good lord; it is more pleasing stuff.
SLY
    What, household stuff?
Page
    It is a kind of history.
SLY
    Well, well see't. Come, madam wife, sit by my side
    and let the world slip: we shall ne'er be younger.

Flourish

ACT I

SCENE I.

Padua. A public place.

Enter LUCENTIO and his man TRANIO

LUCENTIO
    Tranio, since for the great desire I had
    To see fair Padua, nursery of arts,
    I am arrived for fruitful Lombardy,
    The pleasant garden of great Italy;
    And by my father's love and leave am arm'd
    With his good will and thy good company,
    My trusty servant, well approved in all,
    Here let us breathe and haply institute
    A course of learning and ingenious studies.
    Pisa renown'd for grave citizens
    Gave me my being and my father first,
    A merchant of great traffic through the world,
    Vincetino come of Bentivolii.
    Vincetino's son brought up in Florence
    It shall become to serve all hopes conceived,
    To deck his fortune with his virtuous deeds:
    And therefore, Tranio, for the time I study,
    Virtue and that part of philosophy
    Will I apply that treats of happiness
    By virtue specially to be achieved.
    Tell me thy mind; for I have Pisa left
    And am to Padua come, as he that leaves
    A shallow plash to plunge him in the deep
    And with satiety seeks to quench his thirst.
TRANIO
    Mi perdonato, gentle master mine,

I am in all affected as yourself;
Glad that you thus continue your resolve
To suck the sweets of sweet philosophy.
Only, good master, while we do admire
This virtue and this moral discipline,
Let's be no stoics nor no stocks, I pray;
Or so devote to Aristotle's cheques
As Ovid be an outcast quite abjured:
Balk logic with acquaintance that you have
And practise rhetoric in your common talk;
Music and poesy use to quicken you;
The mathematics and the metaphysics,
Fall to them as you find your stomach serves you;
No profit grows where is no pleasure ta'en:
In brief, sir, study what you most affect.

LUCENTIO

Gramercies, Tranio, well dost thou advise.
If, Biondello, thou wert come ashore,
We could at once put us in readiness,
And take a lodging fit to entertain
Such friends as time in Padua shall beget.
But stay a while: what company is this?

TRANIO

Master, some show to welcome us to town.

Enter BAPTISTA, KATHERINA, BIANCA, GREMIO, and
HORTENSIO. LUCENTIO and TRANIO stand by

BAPTISTA

Gentlemen, importune me no farther,
For how I firmly am resolved you know;
That is, not bestow my youngest daughter
Before I have a husband for the elder:
If either of you both love Katharina,
Because I know you well and love you well,

19

Leave shall you have to court her at your pleasure.

GREMIO

[Aside] To cart her rather: she's too rough for me.

There, There, Hortensio, will you any wife?

KATHERINA

I pray you, sir, is it your will

To make a stale of me amongst these mates?

HORTENSIO

Mates, maid! how mean you that? no mates for you,

Unless you were of gentler, milder mould.

KATHERINA

I'faith, sir, you shall never need to fear:

I wis it is not half way to her heart;

But if it were, doubt not her care should be

To comb your noddle with a three-legg'd stool

And paint your face and use you like a fool.

HORTENSIO

From all such devils, good Lord deliver us!

GREMIO

And me too, good Lord!

TRANIO

Hush, master! here's some good pastime toward:

That wench is stark mad or wonderful froward.

LUCENTIO

But in the other's silence do I see

Maid's mild behavior and sobriety.

Peace, Tranio!

TRANIO

Well said, master; mum! and gaze your fill.

BAPTISTA

Gentlemen, that I may soon make good

What I have said, Bianca, get you in:

And let it not displease thee, good Bianca,

For I will love thee ne'er the less, my girl.

KATHERINA

A pretty peat! it is best
Put finger in the eye, an she knew why.

BIANCA

Sister, content you in my discontent.
Sir, to your pleasure humbly I subscribe:
My books and instruments shall be my company,
On them to took and practise by myself.

LUCENTIO

Hark, Tranio! thou may'st hear Minerva speak.

HORTENSIO

Signior Baptista, will you be so strange?
Sorry am I that our good will effects
Bianca's grief.

GREMIO

Why will you mew her up,
Signior Baptista, for this fiend of hell,
And make her bear the penance of her tongue?

BAPTISTA

Gentlemen, content ye; I am resolved:
Go in, Bianca:

Exit BIANCA

And for I know she taketh most delight
In music, instruments and poetry,
Schoolmasters will I keep within my house,
Fit to instruct her youth. If you, Hortensio,
Or Signior Gremio, you, know any such,
Prefer them hither; for to cunning men
I will be very kind, and liberal
To mine own children in good bringing up:
And so farewell. Katharina, you may stay;
For I have more to commune with Bianca.

Exit

KATHERINA
    Why, and I trust I may go too, may I not? What,
    shall I be appointed hours; as though, belike, I
    knew not what to take and what to leave, ha?

Exit

GREMIO
    You may go to the devil's dam: your gifts are so
    good, here's none will hold you. Their love is not
    so great, Hortensio, but we may blow our nails
    together, and fast it fairly out: our cakes dough on
    both sides. Farewell: yet for the love I bear my
    sweet Bianca, if I can by any means light on a fit
    man to teach her that wherein she delights, I will
    wish him to her father.
HORTENSIO
    So will I, Signior Gremio: but a word, I pray.
    Though the nature of our quarrel yet never brooked
    parle, know now, upon advice, it toucheth us both,
    that we may yet again have access to our fair
    mistress and be happy rivals in Bianco's love, to
    labour and effect one thing specially.
GREMIO
    What's that, I pray?
HORTENSIO
    Marry, sir, to get a husband for her sister.
GREMIO
    A husband! a devil.
HORTENSIO
    I say, a husband.
GREMIO
    I say, a devil. Thinkest thou, Hortensio, though

her father be very rich, any man is so very a fool
to be married to hell?

HORTENSIO

Tush, Gremio, though it pass your patience and mine
to endure her loud alarums, why, man, there be good
fellows in the world, an a man could light on them,
would take her with all faults, and money enough.

GREMIO

I cannot tell; but I had as lief take her dowry with
this condition, to be whipped at the high cross
every morning.

HORTENSIO

Faith, as you say, there's small choice in rotten
apples. But come; since this bar in law makes us
friends, it shall be so far forth friendly
maintained all by helping Baptista's eldest daughter
to a husband we set his youngest free for a husband,
and then have to't a fresh. Sweet Bianca! Happy man
be his dole! He that runs fastest gets the ring.
How say you, Signior Gremio?

GREMIO

I am agreed; and would I had given him the best
horse in Padua to begin his wooing that would
thoroughly woo her, wed her and bed her and rid the
house of her! Come on.

Exeunt GREMIO and HORTENSIO

TRANIO

I pray, sir, tell me, is it possible
That love should of a sudden take such hold?

LUCENTIO

O Tranio, till I found it to be true,
I never thought it possible or likely;
But see, while idly I stood looking on,

23

I found the effect of love in idleness:
And now in plainness do confess to thee,
That art to me as secret and as dear
As Anna to the queen of Carthage was,
Tranio, I burn, I pine, I perish, Tranio,
If I achieve not this young modest girl.
Counsel me, Tranio, for I know thou canst;
Assist me, Tranio, for I know thou wilt.

TRANIO

Master, it is no time to chide you now;
Affection is not rated from the heart:
If love have touch'd you, nought remains but so,
'Redime te captum quam queas minimo.'

LUCENTIO

Gramercies, lad, go forward; this contents:
The rest will comfort, for thy counsel's sound.

TRANIO

Master, you look'd so longly on the maid,
Perhaps you mark'd not what's the pith of all.

LUCENTIO

O yes, I saw sweet beauty in her face,
Such as the daughter of Agenor had,
That made great Jove to humble him to her hand.
When with his knees he kiss'd the Cretan strand.

TRANIO

Saw you no more? mark'd you not how her sister
Began to scold and raise up such a storm
That mortal ears might hardly endure the din?

LUCENTIO

Tranio, I saw her coral lips to move
And with her breath she did perfume the air:
Sacred and sweet was all I saw in her.

TRANIO

Nay, then, 'tis time to stir him from his trance.

I pray, awake, sir: if you love the maid,
Bend thoughts and wits to achieve her. Thus it stands:
Her eldest sister is so curst and shrewd
That till the father rid his hands of her,
Master, your love must live a maid at home;
And therefore has he closely mew'd her up,
Because she will not be annoy'd with suitors.
LUCENTIO
Ah, Tranio, what a cruel father's he!
But art thou not advised, he took some care
To get her cunning schoolmasters to instruct her?
TRANIO
Ay, marry, am I, sir; and now 'tis plotted.
LUCENTIO
I have it, Tranio.
TRANIO
Master, for my hand,
Both our inventions meet and jump in one.
LUCENTIO
Tell me thine first.
TRANIO
You will be schoolmaster
And undertake the teaching of the maid:
That's your device.
LUCENTIO
It is: may it be done?
TRANIO
Not possible; for who shall bear your part,
And be in Padua here Vincentio's son,
Keep house and ply his book, welcome his friends,
Visit his countrymen and banquet them?
LUCENTIO
Basta; content thee, for I have it full.
We have not yet been seen in any house,

Nor can we lie distinguish'd by our faces
For man or master; then it follows thus;
Thou shalt be master, Tranio, in my stead,
Keep house and port and servants as I should:
I will some other be, some Florentine,
Some Neapolitan, or meaner man of Pisa.
'Tis hatch'd and shall be so: Tranio, at once
Uncase thee; take my colour'd hat and cloak:
When Biondello comes, he waits on thee;
But I will charm him first to keep his tongue.

TRANIO

So had you need.
In brief, sir, sith it your pleasure is,
And I am tied to be obedient;
For so your father charged me at our parting,
'Be serviceable to my son,' quoth he,
Although I think 'twas in another sense;
I am content to be Lucentio,
Because so well I love Lucentio.

LUCENTIO

Tranio, be so, because Lucentio loves:
And let me be a slave, to achieve that maid
Whose sudden sight hath thrall'd my wounded eye.
Here comes the rogue.

Enter BIONDELLO

Sirrah, where have you been?

BIONDELLO

Where have I been! Nay, how now! where are you?
Master, has my fellow Tranio stolen your clothes? Or
you stolen his? or both? pray, what's the news?

LUCENTIO

Sirrah, come hither: 'tis no time to jest,
And therefore frame your manners to the time.

Your fellow Tranio here, to save my life,
Puts my apparel and my countenance on,
And I for my escape have put on his;
For in a quarrel since I came ashore
I kill'd a man and fear I was descried:
Wait you on him, I charge you, as becomes,
While I make way from hence to save my life:
You understand me?

BIONDELLO

I, sir! ne'er a whit.

LUCENTIO

And not a jot of Tranio in your mouth:
Tranio is changed into Lucentio.

BIONDELLO

The better for him: would I were so too!

TRANIO

So could I, faith, boy, to have the next wish after,
That Lucentio indeed had Baptista's youngest daughter.
But, sirrah, not for my sake, but your master's, I advise
You use your manners discreetly in all kind of
companies:
When I am alone, why, then I am Tranio;
But in all places else your master Lucentio.

LUCENTIO

Tranio, let's go: one thing more rests, that
thyself execute, to make one among these wooers: if
thou ask me why, sufficeth, my reasons are both good
and weighty.

Exeunt

The presenters above speak

First Servant

My lord, you nod; you do not mind the play.

SLY

Yes, by Saint Anne, do I. A good matter, surely:
comes there any more of it?

Page

My lord, 'tis but begun.

SLY

'Tis a very excellent piece of work, madam lady:
would 'twere done!

They sit and mark

SCENE II.

Padua. Before HORTENSIO'S house.

Enter PETRUCHIO and his man GRUMIO

PETRUCHIO

Verona, for a while I take my leave,
To see my friends in Padua, but of all
My best beloved and approved friend,
Hortensio; and I trow this is his house.
Here, sirrah Grumio; knock, I say.

GRUMIO

Knock, sir! whom should I knock? is there man has
rebused your worship?

PETRUCHIO

Villain, I say, knock me here soundly.

GRUMIO

Knock you here, sir! why, sir, what am I, sir, that
I should knock you here, sir?

PETRUCHIO

Villain, I say, knock me at this gate
And rap me well, or I'll knock your knave's pate.

GRUMIO

My master is grown quarrelsome. I should knock
you first,
And then I know after who comes by the worst.
PETRUCHIO
Will it not be?
Faith, sirrah, an you'll not knock, I'll ring it;
I'll try how you can sol, fa, and sing it.

He wrings him by the ears

GRUMIO
Help, masters, help! my master is mad.
PETRUCHIO
Now, knock when I bid you, sirrah villain!

Enter HORTENSIO

HORTENSIO
How now! what's the matter? My old friend Grumio!
and my good friend Petruchio! How do you all at
Verona?
PETRUCHIO
Signior Hortensio, come you to part the fray?
'Con tutto il cuore, ben trovato,' may I say.
HORTENSIO
'Alla nostra casa ben venuto, molto honorato signor
mio Petruchio.' Rise, Grumio, rise: we will compound
this quarrel.
GRUMIO
Nay, 'tis no matter, sir, what he 'leges in Latin.
if this be not a lawful case for me to leave his
service, look you, sir, he bid me knock him and rap
him soundly, sir: well, was it fit for a servant to
use his master so, being perhaps, for aught I see,
two and thirty, a pip out? Whom would to God I had

well knock'd at first, Then had not Grumio come by the worst.

PETRUCHIO

A senseless villain! Good Hortensio,
I bade the rascal knock upon your gate
And could not get him for my heart to do it.

GRUMIO

Knock at the gate! O heavens! Spake you not these
words plain, 'Sirrah, knock me here, rap me here,
knock me well, and knock me soundly'? And come you
now with, 'knocking at the gate'?

PETRUCHIO

Sirrah, be gone, or talk not, I advise you.

HORTENSIO

Petruchio, patience; I am Grumio's pledge:
Why, this's a heavy chance 'twixt him and you,
Your ancient, trusty, pleasant servant Grumio.
And tell me now, sweet friend, what happy gale
Blows you to Padua here from old Verona?

PETRUCHIO

Such wind as scatters young men through the world,
To seek their fortunes farther than at home
Where small experience grows. But in a few,
Signior Hortensio, thus it stands with me:
Antonio, my father, is deceased;
And I have thrust myself into this maze,
Haply to wive and thrive as best I may:
Crowns in my purse I have and goods at home,
And so am come abroad to see the world.

HORTENSIO

Petruchio, shall I then come roundly to thee
And wish thee to a shrewd ill-favour'd wife?
Thou'ldst thank me but a little for my counsel:
And yet I'll promise thee she shall be rich

And very rich: but thou'rt too much my friend,
And I'll not wish thee to her.
PETRUCHIO
Signior Hortensio, 'twixt such friends as we
Few words suffice; and therefore, if thou know
One rich enough to be Petruchio's wife,
As wealth is burden of my wooing dance,
Be she as foul as was Florentius' love,
As old as Sibyl and as curst and shrewd
As Socrates' Xanthippe, or a worse,
She moves me not, or not removes, at least,
Affection's edge in me, were she as rough
As are the swelling Adriatic seas:
I come to wive it wealthily in Padua;
If wealthily, then happily in Padua.
GRUMIO
Nay, look you, sir, he tells you flatly what his
mind is: Why give him gold enough and marry him to
a puppet or an aglet-baby; or an old trot with ne'er
a tooth in her head, though she have as many diseases
as two and fifty horses: why, nothing comes amiss,
so money comes withal.
HORTENSIO
Petruchio, since we are stepp'd thus far in,
I will continue that I broach'd in jest.
I can, Petruchio, help thee to a wife
With wealth enough and young and beauteous,
Brought up as best becomes a gentlewoman:
Her only fault, and that is faults enough,
Is that she is intolerable curst
And shrewd and froward, so beyond all measure
That, were my state far worser than it is,
I would not wed her for a mine of gold.
PETRUCHIO

Hortensio, peace! thou know'st not gold's effect:
Tell me her father's name and 'tis enough;
For I will board her, though she chide as loud
As thunder when the clouds in autumn crack.

HORTENSIO

Her father is Baptista Minola,
An affable and courteous gentleman:
Her name is Katharina Minola,
Renown'd in Padua for her scolding tongue.

PETRUCHIO

I know her father, though I know not her;
And he knew my deceased father well.
I will not sleep, Hortensio, till I see her;
And therefore let me be thus bold with you
To give you over at this first encounter,
Unless you will accompany me thither.

GRUMIO

I pray you, sir, let him go while the humour lasts.
O' my word, an she knew him as well as I do, she
would think scolding would do little good upon him:
she may perhaps call him half a score knaves or so:
why, that's nothing; an he begin once, he'll rail in
his rope-tricks. I'll tell you what sir, an she
stand him but a little, he will throw a figure in
her face and so disfigure her with it that she
shall have no more eyes to see withal than a cat.
You know him not, sir.

HORTENSIO

Tarry, Petruchio, I must go with thee,
For in Baptista's keep my treasure is:
He hath the jewel of my life in hold,
His youngest daughter, beautiful Binaca,
And her withholds from me and other more,
Suitors to her and rivals in my love,

Supposing it a thing impossible,
For those defects I have before rehearsed,
That ever Katharina will be woo'd;
Therefore this order hath Baptista ta'en,
That none shall have access unto Bianca
Till Katharina the curst have got a husband.
GRUMIO
Katharina the curst!
A title for a maid of all titles the worst.
HORTENSIO
Now shall my friend Petruchio do me grace,
And offer me disguised in sober robes
To old Baptista as a schoolmaster
Well seen in music, to instruct Bianca;
That so I may, by this device, at least
Have leave and leisure to make love to her
And unsuspected court her by herself.
GRUMIO
Here's no knavery! See, to beguile the old folks,
how the young folks lay their heads together!

Enter GREMIO, and LUCENTIO disguised

Master, master, look about you: who goes there, ha?
HORTENSIO
Peace, Grumio! it is the rival of my love.
Petruchio, stand by a while.
GRUMIO
A proper stripling and an amorous!
GREMIO
O, very well; I have perused the note.
Hark you, sir: I'll have them very fairly bound:
All books of love, see that at any hand;
And see you read no other lectures to her:
You understand me: over and beside

Signior Baptista's liberality,
I'll mend it with a largess. Take your paper too,
And let me have them very well perfumed
For she is sweeter than perfume itself
To whom they go to. What will you read to her?

LUCENTIO

Whate'er I read to her, I'll plead for you
As for my patron, stand you so assured,
As firmly as yourself were still in place:
Yea, and perhaps with more successful words
Than you, unless you were a scholar, sir.

GREMIO

O this learning, what a thing it is!

GRUMIO

O this woodcock, what an ass it is!

PETRUCHIO

Peace, sirrah!

HORTENSIO

Grumio, mum! God save you, Signior Gremio.

GREMIO

And you are well met, Signior Hortensio.
Trow you whither I am going? To Baptista Minola.
I promised to inquire carefully
About a schoolmaster for the fair Bianca:
And by good fortune I have lighted well
On this young man, for learning and behavior
Fit for her turn, well read in poetry
And other books, good ones, I warrant ye.

HORTENSIO

'Tis well; and I have met a gentleman
Hath promised me to help me to another,
A fine musician to instruct our mistress;
So shall I no whit be behind in duty
To fair Bianca, so beloved of me.

GREMIO
　Beloved of me; and that my deeds shall prove.
GRUMIO
　And that his bags shall prove.
HORTENSIO
　Gremio, 'tis now no time to vent our love:
　Listen to me, and if you speak me fair,
　I'll tell you news indifferent good for either.
　Here is a gentleman whom by chance I met,
　Upon agreement from us to his liking,
　Will undertake to woo curst Katharina,
　Yea, and to marry her, if her dowry please.
GREMIO
　So said, so done, is well.
　Hortensio, have you told him all her faults?
PETRUCHIO
　I know she is an irksome brawling scold:
　If that be all, masters, I hear no harm.
GREMIO
　No, say'st me so, friend? What countryman?
PETRUCHIO
　Born in Verona, old Antonio's son:
　My father dead, my fortune lives for me;
　And I do hope good days and long to see.
GREMIO
　O sir, such a life, with such a wife, were strange!
　But if you have a stomach, to't i' God's name:
　You shall have me assisting you in all.
　But will you woo this wild-cat?
PETRUCHIO
　Will I live?
GRUMIO
　Will he woo her? ay, or I'll hang her.
PETRUCHIO

Why came I hither but to that intent?
Think you a little din can daunt mine ears?
Have I not in my time heard lions roar?
Have I not heard the sea puff'd up with winds
Rage like an angry boar chafed with sweat?
Have I not heard great ordnance in the field,
And heaven's artillery thunder in the skies?
Have I not in a pitched battle heard
Loud 'larums, neighing steeds, and trumpets' clang?
And do you tell me of a woman's tongue,
That gives not half so great a blow to hear
As will a chestnut in a farmer's fire?
Tush, tush! fear boys with bugs.

GRUMIO

For he fears none.

GREMIO

Hortensio, hark:
This gentleman is happily arrived,
My mind presumes, for his own good and ours.

HORTENSIO

I promised we would be contributors
And bear his charging of wooing, whatsoe'er.

GREMIO

And so we will, provided that he win her.

GRUMIO

I would I were as sure of a good dinner.

Enter TRANIO brave, and BIONDELLO

TRANIO

Gentlemen, God save you. If I may be bold,
Tell me, I beseech you, which is the readiest way
To the house of Signior Baptista Minola?

BIONDELLO

He that has the two fair daughters: is't he you mean?

TRANIO
  Even he, Biondello.
GREMIO
  Hark you, sir; you mean not her to--
TRANIO
  Perhaps, him and her, sir: what have you to do?
PETRUCHIO
  Not her that chides, sir, at any hand, I pray.
TRANIO
  I love no chiders, sir. Biondello, let's away.
LUCENTIO
  Well begun, Tranio.
HORTENSIO
  Sir, a word ere you go;
  Are you a suitor to the maid you talk of, yea or no?
TRANIO
  And if I be, sir, is it any offence?
GREMIO
  No; if without more words you will get you hence.
TRANIO
  Why, sir, I pray, are not the streets as free
  For me as for you?
GREMIO
  But so is not she.
TRANIO
  For what reason, I beseech you?
GREMIO
  For this reason, if you'll know,
  That she's the choice love of Signior Gremio.
HORTENSIO
  That she's the chosen of Signior Hortensio.
TRANIO
  Softly, my masters! if you be gentlemen,
  Do me this right; hear me with patience.

Baptista is a noble gentleman,
To whom my father is not all unknown;
And were his daughter fairer than she is,
She may more suitors have and me for one.
Fair Leda's daughter had a thousand wooers;
Then well one more may fair Bianca have:
And so she shall; Lucentio shall make one,
Though Paris came in hope to speed alone.

GREMIO
What! this gentleman will out-talk us all.

LUCENTIO
Sir, give him head: I know he'll prove a jade.

PETRUCHIO
Hortensio, to what end are all these words?

HORTENSIO
Sir, let me be so bold as ask you,
Did you yet ever see Baptista's daughter?

TRANIO
No, sir; but hear I do that he hath two,
The one as famous for a scolding tongue
As is the other for beauteous modesty.

PETRUCHIO
Sir, sir, the first's for me; let her go by.

GREMIO
Yea, leave that labour to great Hercules;
And let it be more than Alcides' twelve.

PETRUCHIO
Sir, understand you this of me in sooth:
The younges t daughter whom you hearken for
Her father keeps from all access of suitors,
And will not promise her to any man
Until the elder sister first be wed:
The younger then is free and not before.

TRANIO

If it be so, sir, that you are the man
Must stead us all and me amongst the rest,
And if you break the ice and do this feat,
Achieve the elder, set the younger free
For our access, whose hap shall be to have her
Will not so graceless be to be ingrate.

HORTENSIO

Sir, you say well and well you do conceive;
And since you do profess to be a suitor,
You must, as we do, gratify this gentleman,
To whom we all rest generally beholding.

TRANIO

Sir, I shall not be slack: in sign whereof,
Please ye we may contrive this afternoon,
And quaff carouses to our mistress' health,
And do as adversaries do in law,
Strive mightily, but eat and drink as friends.

GRUMIO BIONDELLO

O excellent motion! Fellows, let's be gone.

HORTENSIO

The motion's good indeed and be it so,
Petruchio, I shall be your ben venuto.

Exeunt

ACT II

SCENE I.

Padua. A room in BAPTISTA'S house.

Enter KATHERINA and BIANCA

BIANCA
  Good sister, wrong me not, nor wrong yourself,
  To make a bondmaid and a slave of me;
  That I disdain: but for these other gawds,
  Unbind my hands, I'll pull them off myself,
  Yea, all my raiment, to my petticoat;
  Or what you will command me will I do,
  So well I know my duty to my elders.

KATHERINA
  Of all thy suitors, here I charge thee, tell
  Whom thou lovest best: see thou dissemble not.

BIANCA
  Believe me, sister, of all the men alive
  I never yet beheld that special face
  Which I could fancy more than any other.

KATHERINA
  Minion, thou liest. Is't not Hortensio?

BIANCA
  If you affect him, sister, here I swear
  I'll plead for you myself, but you shall have
  him.

KATHERINA
  O then, belike, you fancy riches more:
  You will have Gremio to keep you fair.

BIANCA
  Is it for him you do envy me so?
  Nay then you jest, and now I well perceive

You have but jested with me all this while:
I prithee, sister Kate, untie my hands.
KATHERINA
If that be jest, then all the rest was so.

Strikes her

Enter BAPTISTA

BAPTISTA
Why, how now, dame! whence grows this insolence?
Bianca, stand aside. Poor girl! she weeps.
Go ply thy needle; meddle not with her.
For shame, thou helding of a devilish spirit,
Why dost thou wrong her that did ne'er wrong thee?
When did she cross thee with a bitter word?
KATHERINA
Her silence flouts me, and I'll be revenged.

Flies after BIANCA

BAPTISTA
What, in my sight? Bianca, get thee in.

Exit BIANCA

KATHERINA
What, will you not suffer me? Nay, now I see
She is your treasure, she must have a husband;
I must dance bare-foot on her wedding day
And for your love to her lead apes in hell.
Talk not to me: I will go sit and weep
Till I can find occasion of revenge.

Exit

BAPTISTA

Was ever gentleman thus grieved as I?
But who comes here?

*Enter GREMIO, LUCENTIO in the habit of a mean man;
PETRUCHIO, with HORTENSIO as a musician; and
TRANIO, with BIONDELLO bearing a lute and books*

GREMIO

Good morrow, neighbour Baptista.

BAPTISTA

Good morrow, neighbour Gremio.
God save you, gentlemen!

PETRUCHIO

And you, good sir! Pray, have you not a daughter
Call'd Katharina, fair and virtuous?

BAPTISTA

I have a daughter, sir, called Katharina.

GREMIO

You are too blunt: go to it orderly.

PETRUCHIO

You wrong me, Signior Gremio: give me leave.
I am a gentleman of Verona, sir,
That, hearing of her beauty and her wit,
Her affability and bashful modesty,
Her wondrous qualities and mild behavior,
Am bold to show myself a forward guest
Within your house, to make mine eye the witness
Of that report which I so oft have heard.
And, for an entrance to my entertainment,
I do present you with a man of mine,

Presenting HORTENSIO

Cunning in music and the mathematics,

To instruct her fully in those sciences,
Whereof I know she is not ignorant:
Accept of him, or else you do me wrong:
His name is Licio, born in Mantua.

BAPTISTA

You're welcome, sir; and he, for your good sake.
But for my daughter Katharina, this I know,
She is not for your turn, the more my grief.

PETRUCHIO

I see you do not mean to part with her,
Or else you like not of my company.

BAPTISTA

Mistake me not; I speak but as I find.
Whence are you, sir? what may I call your name?

PETRUCHIO

Petruchio is my name; Antonio's son,
A man well known throughout all Italy.

BAPTISTA

I know him well: you are welcome for his sake.

GREMIO

Saving your tale, Petruchio, I pray,
Let us, that are poor petitioners, speak too:
Baccare! you are marvellous forward.

PETRUCHIO

O, pardon me, Signior Gremio; I would fain be doing.

GREMIO

I doubt it not, sir; but you will curse your
wooing. Neighbour, this is a gift very grateful, I am
sure of it. To express the like kindness, myself,
that have been more kindly beholding to you than
any, freely give unto you this young scholar,

Presenting LUCENTIO

that hath been long studying at Rheims; as cunning

43

in Greek, Latin, and other languages, as the other
in music and mathematics: his name is Cambio; pray,
accept his service.
BAPTISTA
A thousand thanks, Signior Gremio.
Welcome, good Cambio.

To TRANIO

But, gentle sir, methinks you walk like a stranger:
may I be so bold to know the cause of your coming?
TRANIO
Pardon me, sir, the boldness is mine own,
That, being a stranger in this city here,
Do make myself a suitor to your daughter,
Unto Bianca, fair and virtuous.
Nor is your firm resolve unknown to me,
In the preferment of the eldest sister.
This liberty is all that I request,
That, upon knowledge of my parentage,
I may have welcome 'mongst the rest that woo
And free access and favour as the rest:
And, toward the education of your daughters,
I here bestow a simple instrument,
And this small packet of Greek and Latin books:
If you accept them, then their worth is great.
BAPTISTA
Lucentio is your name; of whence, I pray?
TRANIO
Of Pisa, sir; son to Vincentio.
BAPTISTA
A mighty man of Pisa; by report
I know him well: you are very welcome, sir,
Take you the lute, and you the set of books;
You shall go see your pupils presently.

Holla, within!

Enter a Servant

Sirrah, lead these gentlemen
To my daughters; and tell them both,
These are their tutors: bid them use them well.

Exit Servant, with LUCENTIO and HORTENSIO,
BIONDELLO following

We will go walk a little in the orchard,
And then to dinner. You are passing welcome,
And so I pray you all to think yourselves.
PETRUCHIO
    Signior Baptista, my business asketh haste,
    And every day I cannot come to woo.
    You knew my father well, and in him me,
    Left solely heir to all his lands and goods,
    Which I have better'd rather than decreased:
    Then tell me, if I get your daughter's love,
    What dowry shall I have with her to wife?
BAPTISTA
    After my death the one half of my lands,
    And in possession twenty thousand crowns.
PETRUCHIO
    And, for that dowry, I'll assure her of
    Her widowhood, be it that she survive me,
    In all my lands and leases whatsoever:
    Let specialties be therefore drawn between us,
    That covenants may be kept on either hand.
BAPTISTA
    Ay, when the special thing is well obtain'd,
    That is, her love; for that is all in all.
PETRUCHIO

Why, that is nothing: for I tell you, father,
I am as peremptory as she proud-minded;
And where two raging fires meet together
They do consume the thing that feeds their fury:
Though little fire grows great with little wind,
Yet extreme gusts will blow out fire and all:
So I to her and so she yields to me;
For I am rough and woo not like a babe.
BAPTISTA
Well mayst thou woo, and happy be thy speed!
But be thou arm'd for some unhappy words.
PETRUCHIO
Ay, to the proof; as mountains are for winds,
That shake not, though they blow perpetually.

Re-enter HORTENSIO, with his head broke

BAPTISTA
How now, my friend! why dost thou look so pale?
HORTENSIO
For fear, I promise you, if I look pale.
BAPTISTA
What, will my daughter prove a good musician?
HORTENSIO
I think she'll sooner prove a soldier
Iron may hold with her, but never lutes.
BAPTISTA
Why, then thou canst not break her to the lute?
HORTENSIO
Why, no; for she hath broke the lute to me.
I did but tell her she mistook her frets,
And bow'd her hand to teach her fingering;
When, with a most impatient devilish spirit,
'Frets, call you these?' quoth she; 'I'll fume
with them:'

46

And, with that word, she struck me on the head,
And through the instrument my pate made way;
And there I stood amazed for a while,
As on a pillory, looking through the lute;
While she did call me rascal fiddler
And twangling Jack; with twenty such vile terms,
As had she studied to misuse me so.

PETRUCHIO
Now, by the world, it is a lusty wench;
I love her ten times more than e'er I did:
O, how I long to have some chat with her!

BAPTISTA
Well, go with me and be not so discomfited:
Proceed in practise with my younger daughter;
She's apt to learn and thankful for good turns.
Signior Petruchio, will you go with us,
Or shall I send my daughter Kate to you?

PETRUCHIO
I pray you do.

Exeunt all but PETRUCHIO

I will attend her here,
And woo her with some spirit when she comes.
Say that she rail; why then I'll tell her plain
She sings as sweetly as a nightingale:
Say that she frown, I'll say she looks as clear
As morning roses newly wash'd with dew:
Say she be mute and will not speak a word;
Then I'll commend her volubility,
And say she uttereth piercing eloquence:
If she do bid me pack, I'll give her thanks,
As though she bid me stay by her a week:
If she deny to wed, I'll crave the day
When I shall ask the banns and when be married.

But here she comes; and now, Petruchio, speak.

Enter KATHERINA

Good morrow, Kate; for that's your name, I hear.
KATHERINA
Well have you heard, but something hard of hearing:
They call me Katharina that do talk of me.
PETRUCHIO
You lie, in faith; for you are call'd plain Kate,
And bonny Kate and sometimes Kate the curst;
But Kate, the prettiest Kate in Christendom
Kate of Kate Hall, my super-dainty Kate,
For dainties are all Kates, and therefore, Kate,
Take this of me, Kate of my consolation;
Hearing thy mildness praised in every town,
Thy virtues spoke of, and thy beauty sounded,
Yet not so deeply as to thee belongs,
Myself am moved to woo thee for my wife.
KATHERINA
Moved! in good time: let him that moved you hither
Remove you hence: I knew you at the first
You were a moveable.
PETRUCHIO
Why, what's a moveable?
KATHERINA
A join'd-stool.
PETRUCHIO
Thou hast hit it: come, sit on me.
KATHERINA
Asses are made to bear, and so are you.
PETRUCHIO
Women are made to bear, and so are you.
KATHERINA
No such jade as you, if me you mean.

PETRUCHIO
  Alas! good Kate, I will not burden thee;
  For, knowing thee to be but young and light--
KATHERINA
  Too light for such a swain as you to catch;
  And yet as heavy as my weight should be.
PETRUCHIO
  Should be! should--buzz!
KATHERINA
  Well ta'en, and like a buzzard.
PETRUCHIO
  O slow-wing'd turtle! shall a buzzard take thee?
KATHERINA
  Ay, for a turtle, as he takes a buzzard.
PETRUCHIO
  Come, come, you wasp; i' faith, you are too angry.
KATHERINA
  If I be waspish, best beware my sting.
PETRUCHIO
  My remedy is then, to pluck it out.
KATHERINA
  Ay, if the fool could find it where it lies,
PETRUCHIO
  Who knows not where a wasp does
  wear his sting? In his tail.
KATHERINA
  In his tongue.
PETRUCHIO
  Whose tongue?
KATHERINA
  Yours, if you talk of tails: and so farewell.
PETRUCHIO
  What, with my tongue in your tail? nay, come again,
  Good Kate; I am a gentleman.

KATHERINA
  That I'll try.

She strikes him

PETRUCHIO
  I swear I'll cuff you, if you strike again.
KATHERINA
  So may you lose your arms:
  If you strike me, you are no gentleman;
  And if no gentleman, why then no arms.
PETRUCHIO
  A herald, Kate? O, put me in thy books!
KATHERINA
  What is your crest? a coxcomb?
PETRUCHIO
  A combless cock, so Kate will be my hen.
KATHERINA
  No cock of mine; you crow too like a craven.
PETRUCHIO
  Nay, come, Kate, come; you must not look so sour.
KATHERINA
  It is my fashion, when I see a crab.
PETRUCHIO
  Why, here's no crab; and therefore look not sour.
KATHERINA
  There is, there is.
PETRUCHIO
  Then show it me.
KATHERINA
  Had I a glass, I would.
PETRUCHIO
  What, you mean my face?
KATHERINA
  Well aim'd of such a young one.

PETRUCHIO
Now, by Saint George, I am too young for you.
KATHERINA
Yet you are wither'd.
PETRUCHIO
'Tis with cares.
KATHERINA
I care not.
PETRUCHIO
Nay, hear you, Kate: in sooth you scape not so.
KATHERINA
I chafe you, if I tarry: let me go.
PETRUCHIO
No, not a whit: I find you passing gentle.
'Twas told me you were rough and coy and sullen,
And now I find report a very liar;
For thou are pleasant, gamesome, passing courteous,
But slow in speech, yet sweet as spring-time flowers:
Thou canst not frown, thou canst not look askance,
Nor bite the lip, as angry wenches will,
Nor hast thou pleasure to be cross in talk,
But thou with mildness entertain'st thy wooers,
With gentle conference, soft and affable.
Why does the world report that Kate doth limp?
O slanderous world! Kate like the hazel-twig
Is straight and slender and as brown in hue
As hazel nuts and sweeter than the kernels.
O, let me see thee walk: thou dost not halt.
KATHERINA
Go, fool, and whom thou keep'st command.
PETRUCHIO
Did ever Dian so become a grove
As Kate this chamber with her princely gait?
O, be thou Dian, and let her be Kate;

And then let Kate be chaste and Dian sportful!
KATHERINA
Where did you study all this goodly speech?
PETRUCHIO
It is extempore, from my mother-wit.
KATHERINA
A witty mother! witless else her son.
PETRUCHIO
Am I not wise?
KATHERINA
Yes; keep you warm.
PETRUCHIO
Marry, so I mean, sweet Katharina, in thy bed:
And therefore, setting all this chat aside,
Thus in plain terms: your father hath consented
That you shall be my wife; your dowry 'greed on;
And, Will you, nill you, I will marry you.
Now, Kate, I am a husband for your turn;
For, by this light, whereby I see thy beauty,
Thy beauty, that doth make me like thee well,
Thou must be married to no man but me;
For I am he am born to tame you Kate,
And bring you from a wild Kate to a Kate
Conformable as other household Kates.
Here comes your father: never make denial;
I must and will have Katharina to my wife.

Re-enter BAPTISTA, GREMIO, and TRANIO

BAPTISTA
Now, Signior Petruchio, how speed you with my
daughter?
PETRUCHIO
How but well, sir? how but well?
It were impossible I should speed amiss.

BAPTISTA

Why, how now, daughter Katharina! in your dumps?

KATHERINA

Call you me daughter? now, I promise you
You have show'd a tender fatherly regard,
To wish me wed to one half lunatic;
A mad-cup ruffian and a swearing Jack,
That thinks with oaths to face the matter out.

PETRUCHIO

Father, 'tis thus: yourself and all the world,
That talk'd of her, have talk'd amiss of her:
If she be curst, it is for policy,
For she's not froward, but modest as the dove;
She is not hot, but temperate as the morn;
For patience she will prove a second Grissel,
And Roman Lucrece for her chastity:
And to conclude, we have 'greed so well together,
That upon Sunday is the wedding-day.

KATHERINA

I'll see thee hang'd on Sunday first.

GREMIO

Hark, Petruchio; she says she'll see thee
hang'd first.

TRANIO

Is this your speeding? nay, then, good night our part!

PETRUCHIO

Be patient, gentlemen; I choose her for myself:
If she and I be pleased, what's that to you?
'Tis bargain'd 'twixt us twain, being alone,
That she shall still be curst in company.
I tell you, 'tis incredible to believe
How much she loves me: O, the kindest Kate!
She hung about my neck; and kiss on kiss
She vied so fast, protesting oath on oath,

That in a twink she won me to her love.
O, you are novices! 'tis a world to see,
How tame, when men and women are alone,
A meacock wretch can make the curstest shrew.
Give me thy hand, Kate: I will unto Venice,
To buy apparel 'gainst the wedding-day.
Provide the feast, father, and bid the guests;
I will be sure my Katharina shall be fine.

BAPTISTA

I know not what to say: but give me your hands;
God send you joy, Petruchio! 'tis a match.

GREMIO and TRANIO

Amen, say we: we will be witnesses.

PETRUCHIO

Father, and wife, and gentlemen, adieu;
I will to Venice; Sunday comes apace:
We will have rings and things and fine array;
And kiss me, Kate, we will be married o'Sunday.

Exeunt PETRUCHIO and KATHERINA severally

GREMIO

Was ever match clapp'd up so suddenly?

BAPTISTA

Faith, gentlemen, now I play a merchant's part,
And venture madly on a desperate mart.

TRANIO

'Twas a commodity lay fretting by you:
'Twill bring you gain, or perish on the seas.

BAPTISTA

The gain I seek is, quiet in the match.

GREMIO

No doubt but he hath got a quiet catch.
But now, Baptists, to your younger daughter:
Now is the day we long have looked for:

I am your neighbour, and was suitor first.
TRANIO
    And I am one that love Bianca more
    Than words can witness, or your thoughts can guess.
GREMIO
    Youngling, thou canst not love so dear as I.
TRANIO
    Graybeard, thy love doth freeze.
GREMIO
    But thine doth fry.
    Skipper, stand back: 'tis age that nourisheth.
TRANIO
    But youth in ladies' eyes that flourisheth.
BAPTISTA
    Content you, gentlemen: I will compound this strife:
    'Tis deeds must win the prize; and he of both
    That can assure my daughter greatest dower
    Shall have my Bianca's love.
    Say, Signior Gremio, What can you assure her?
GREMIO
    First, as you know, my house within the city
    Is richly furnished with plate and gold;
    Basins and ewers to lave her dainty hands;
    My hangings all of Tyrian tapestry;
    In ivory coffers I have stuff'd my crowns;
    In cypress chests my arras counterpoints,
    Costly apparel, tents, and canopies,
    Fine linen, Turkey cushions boss'd with pearl,
    Valance of Venice gold in needlework,
    Pewter and brass and all things that belong
    To house or housekeeping: then, at my farm
    I have a hundred milch-kine to the pail,
    Sixscore fat oxen standing in my stalls,
    And all things answerable to this portion.

Myself am struck in years, I must confess;
And if I die to-morrow, this is hers,
If whilst I live she will be only mine.
TRANIO
That 'only' came well in. Sir, list to me:
I am my father's heir and only son:
If I may have your daughter to my wife,
I'll leave her houses three or four as good,
Within rich Pisa walls, as any one
Old Signior Gremio has in Padua;
Besides two thousand ducats by the year
Of fruitful land, all which shall be her jointure.
What, have I pinch'd you, Signior Gremio?
GREMIO
Two thousand ducats by the year of land!
My land amounts not to so much in all:
That she shall have; besides an argosy
That now is lying in Marseilles' road.
What, have I choked you with an argosy?
TRANIO
Gremio, 'tis known my father hath no less
Than three great argosies; besides two galliases,
And twelve tight galleys: these I will assure her,
And twice as much, whate'er thou offer'st next.
GREMIO
Nay, I have offer'd all, I have no more;
And she can have no more than all I have:
If you like me, she shall have me and mine.
TRANIO
Why, then the maid is mine from all the world,
By your firm promise: Gremio is out-vied.
BAPTISTA
I must confess your offer is the best;
And, let your father make her the assurance,

She is your own; else, you must pardon me,
if you should die before him, where's her dower?

TRANIO

That's but a cavil: he is old, I young.

GREMIO

And may not young men die, as well as old?

BAPTISTA

Well, gentlemen,
I am thus resolved: on Sunday next you know
My daughter Katharina is to be married:
Now, on the Sunday following, shall Bianca
Be bride to you, if you this assurance;
If not, Signior Gremio:
And so, I take my leave, and thank you both.

GREMIO

Adieu, good neighbour.

Exit BAPTISTA

Now I fear thee not:
Sirrah young gamester, your father were a fool
To give thee all, and in his waning age
Set foot under thy table: tut, a toy!
An old Italian fox is not so kind, my boy.

Exit

TRANIO

A vengeance on your crafty wither'd hide!
Yet I have faced it with a card of ten.
'Tis in my head to do my master good:
I see no reason but supposed Lucentio
Must get a father, call'd 'supposed Vincentio;'
And that's a wonder: fathers commonly
Do get their children; but in this case of wooing,
A child shall get a sire, if I fail not of my cunning.

Exit

ACT III

SCENE I.

Padua. BAPTISTA'S house.

Enter LUCENTIO, HORTENSIO, and BIANCA

LUCENTIO

 Fiddler, forbear; you grow too forward, sir:
 Have you so soon forgot the entertainment
 Her sister Katharina welcomed you withal?

HORTENSIO

 But, wrangling pedant, this is
 The patroness of heavenly harmony:
 Then give me leave to have prerogative;
 And when in music we have spent an hour,
 Your lecture shall have leisure for as much.

LUCENTIO

 Preposterous ass, that never read so far
 To know the cause why music was ordain'd!
 Was it not to refresh the mind of man
 After his studies or his usual pain?
 Then give me leave to read philosophy,
 And while I pause, serve in your harmony.

HORTENSIO

 Sirrah, I will not bear these braves of thine.

BIANCA

 Why, gentlemen, you do me double wrong,
 To strive for that which resteth in my choice:
 I am no breeching scholar in the schools;
 I'll not be tied to hours nor 'pointed times,
 But learn my lessons as I please myself.
 And, to cut off all strife, here sit we down:
 Take you your instrument, play you the whiles;

58

His lecture will be done ere you have tuned.

HORTENSIO

You'll leave his lecture when I am in tune?

LUCENTIO

That will be never: tune your instrument.

BIANCA

Where left we last?

LUCENTIO

Here, madam:
'Hic ibat Simois; hic est Sigeia tellus;
Hic steterat Priami regia celsa senis.'

BIANCA

Construe them.

LUCENTIO

'Hic ibat,' as I told you before, 'Simois,' I am
Lucentio, 'hic est,' son unto Vincentio of Pisa,
'Sigeia tellus,' disguised thus to get your love;
'Hic steterat,' and that Lucentio that comes
a-wooing, 'Priami,' is my man Tranio, 'regia,'
bearing my port, 'celsa senis,' that we might
beguile the old pantaloon.

HORTENSIO

Madam, my instrument's in tune.

BIANCA

Let's hear. O fie! the treble jars.

LUCENTIO

Spit in the hole, man, and tune again.

BIANCA

Now let me see if I can construe it: 'Hic ibat
Simois,' I know you not, 'hic est Sigeia tellus,' I
trust you not; 'Hic steterat Priami,' take heed
he hear us not, 'regia,' presume not, 'celsa senis,'
despair not.

HORTENSIO

Madam, 'tis now in tune.
LUCENTIO
All but the base.
HORTENSIO
The base is right; 'tis the base knave that jars.

Aside

How fiery and forward our pedant is!
Now, for my life, the knave doth court my love:
Pedascule, I'll watch you better yet.
BIANCA
In time I may believe, yet I mistrust.
LUCENTIO
Mistrust it not: for, sure, AEacides
Was Ajax, call'd so from his grandfather.
BIANCA
I must believe my master; else, I promise you,
I should be arguing still upon that doubt:
But let it rest. Now, Licio, to you:
Good masters, take it not unkindly, pray,
That I have been thus pleasant with you both.
HORTENSIO
You may go walk, and give me leave a while:
My lessons make no music in three parts.
LUCENTIO
Are you so formal, sir? well, I must wait,

Aside

And watch withal; for, but I be deceived,
Our fine musician groweth amorous.
HORTENSIO
Madam, before you touch the instrument,
To learn the order of my fingering,

I must begin with rudiments of art;
To teach you gamut in a briefer sort,
More pleasant, pithy and effectual,
Than hath been taught by any of my trade:
And there it is in writing, fairly drawn.
BIANCA
Why, I am past my gamut long ago.
HORTENSIO
Yet read the gamut of Hortensio.
BIANCA
[Reads] "Gamut' I am, the ground of all accord,
'A re,' to Plead Hortensio's passion;
'B mi,' Bianca, take him for thy lord,
'C fa ut,' that loves with all affection:
'D sol re,' one clef, two notes have I:
'E la mi,' show pity, or I die.'
Call you this gamut? tut, I like it not:
Old fashions please me best; I am not so nice,
To change true rules for old inventions.

Enter a Servant

Servant
Mistress, your father prays you leave your books
And help to dress your sister's chamber up:
You know to-morrow is the wedding-day.
BIANCA
Farewell, sweet masters both; I must be gone.

Exeunt BIANCA and Servant

LUCENTIO
Faith, mistress, then I have no cause to stay.

Exit

61

HORTENSIO

But I have cause to pry into this pedant:
Methinks he looks as though he were in love:
Yet if thy thoughts, Bianca, be so humble
To cast thy wandering eyes on every stale,
Seize thee that list: if once I find thee ranging,
Hortensio will be quit with thee by changing.

Exit

SCENE II.

Padua. Before BAPTISTA'S house.

Enter BAPTISTA, GREMIO, TRANIO, KATHERINA,
BIANCA, LUCENTIO, and others, attendants

BAPTISTA

[To TRANIO] Signior Lucentio, this is the
'pointed day.
That Katharina and Petruchio should be married,
And yet we hear not of our son-in-law.
What will be said? what mockery will it be,
To want the bridegroom when the priest attends
To speak the ceremonial rites of marriage!
What says Lucentio to this shame of ours?
KATHERINA

No shame but mine: I must, forsooth, be forced
To give my hand opposed against my heart
Unto a mad-brain rudesby full of spleen;
Who woo'd in haste and means to wed at leisure.
I told you, I, he was a frantic fool,
Hiding his bitter jests in blunt behavior:
And, to be noted for a merry man,
He'll woo a thousand, 'point the day of marriage,
Make feasts, invite friends, and proclaim the banns;

Yet never means to wed where he hath woo'd.
Now must the world point at poor Katharina,
And say, 'Lo, there is mad Petruchio's wife,
If it would please him come and marry her!'
TRANIO
Patience, good Katharina, and Baptista too.
Upon my life, Petruchio means but well,
Whatever fortune stays him from his word:
Though he be blunt, I know him passing wise;
Though he be merry, yet withal he's honest.
KATHERINA
Would Katharina had never seen him though!

Exit weeping, followed by BIANCA and others

BAPTISTA
Go, girl; I cannot blame thee now to weep;
For such an injury would vex a very saint,
Much more a shrew of thy impatient humour.

Enter BIONDELLO

BIONDELLO
Master, master! news, old news, and such news as
you never heard of!
BAPTISTA
Is it new and old too? how may that be?
BIONDELLO
Why, is it not news, to hear of Petruchio's coming?
BAPTISTA
Is he come?
BIONDELLO
Why, no, sir.
BAPTISTA
What then?

BIONDELLO
  He is coming.
BAPTISTA
  When will he be here?
BIONDELLO
  When he stands where I am and sees you there.
TRANIO
  But say, what to thine old news?
BIONDELLO
  Why, Petruchio is coming in a new hat and an old
  jerkin, a pair of old breeches thrice turned, a pair
  of boots that have been candle-cases, one buckled,
  another laced, an old rusty sword ta'en out of the
  town-armory, with a broken hilt, and chapeless;
  with two broken points: his horse hipped with an
  old mothy saddle and stirrups of no kindred;
  besides, possessed with the glanders and like to mose
  in the chine; troubled with the lampass, infected
  with the fashions, full of wingdalls, sped with
  spavins, rayed with yellows, past cure of the fives,
  stark spoiled with the staggers, begnawn with the
  bots, swayed in the back and shoulder-shotten;
  near-legged before and with, a half-chequed bit
  and a head-stall of sheeps leather which, being
  restrained to keep him from stumbling, hath been
  often burst and now repaired with knots; one girth
  six time pieced and a woman's crupper of velure,
  which hath two letters for her name fairly set down
  in studs, and here and there pieced with packthread.
BAPTISTA
  Who comes with him?
BIONDELLO
  O, sir, his lackey, for all the world caparisoned
  like the horse; with a linen stock on one leg and a

kersey boot-hose on the other, gartered with a red
and blue list; an old hat and 'the humour of forty
fancies' pricked in't for a feather: a monster, a
very monster in apparel, and not like a Christian
footboy or a gentleman's lackey.

TRANIO

'Tis some odd humour pricks him to this fashion;
Yet oftentimes he goes but mean-apparell'd.

BAPTISTA

I am glad he's come, howsoe'er he comes.

BIONDELLO

Why, sir, he comes not.

BAPTISTA

Didst thou not say he comes?

BIONDELLO

Who? that Petruchio came?

BAPTISTA

Ay, that Petruchio came.

BIONDELLO

No, sir, I say his horse comes, with him on his back.

BAPTISTA

Why, that's all one.

BIONDELLO

Nay, by Saint Jamy,
I hold you a penny,
A horse and a man
Is more than one,
And yet not many.

Enter PETRUCHIO and GRUMIO

PETRUCHIO

Come, where be these gallants? who's at home?

BAPTISTA

You are welcome, sir.

PETRUCHIO
And yet I come not well.
BAPTISTA
And yet you halt not.
TRANIO
Not so well apparell'd
As I wish you were.
PETRUCHIO
Were it better, I should rush in thus.
But where is Kate? where is my lovely bride?
How does my father? Gentles, methinks you frown:
And wherefore gaze this goodly company,
As if they saw some wondrous monument,
Some comet or unusual prodigy?
BAPTISTA
Why, sir, you know this is your wedding-day:
First were we sad, fearing you would not come;
Now sadder, that you come so unprovided.
Fie, doff this habit, shame to your estate,
An eye-sore to our solemn festival!
TRANIO
And tells us, what occasion of import
Hath all so long detain'd you from your wife,
And sent you hither so unlike yourself?
PETRUCHIO
Tedious it were to tell, and harsh to hear:
Sufficeth I am come to keep my word,
Though in some part enforced to digress;
Which, at more leisure, I will so excuse
As you shall well be satisfied withal.
But where is Kate? I stay too long from her:
The morning wears, 'tis time we were at church.
TRANIO
See not your bride in these unreverent robes:

66

Go to my chamber; Put on clothes of mine.
PETRUCHIO
　Not I, believe me: thus I'll visit her.
BAPTISTA
　But thus, I trust, you will not marry her.
PETRUCHIO
　Good sooth, even thus; therefore ha' done with words:
　To me she's married, not unto my clothes:
　Could I repair what she will wear in me,
　As I can change these poor accoutrements,
　'Twere well for Kate and better for myself.
　But what a fool am I to chat with you,
　When I should bid good morrow to my bride,
　And seal the title with a lovely kiss!

Exeunt PETRUCHIO and GRUMIO

TRANIO
　He hath some meaning in his mad attire:
　We will persuade him, be it possible,
　To put on better ere he go to church.
BAPTISTA
　I'll after him, and see the event of this.

Exeunt BAPTISTA, GREMIO, and attendants

TRANIO
　But to her love concerneth us to add
　Her father's liking: which to bring to pass,
　As I before unparted to your worship,
　I am to get a man,--whate'er he be,
　It skills not much. we'll fit him to our turn,--
　And he shall be Vincentio of Pisa;
　And make assurance here in Padua
　Of greater sums than I have promised.

So shall you quietly enjoy your hope,
And marry sweet Bianca with consent.
LUCENTIO
Were it not that my fellow-school-master
Doth watch Bianca's steps so narrowly,
'Twere good, methinks, to steal our marriage;
Which once perform'd, let all the world say no,
I'll keep mine own, despite of all the world.
TRANIO
That by degrees we mean to look into,
And watch our vantage in this business:
We'll over-reach the greybeard, Gremio,
The narrow-prying father, Minola,
The quaint musician, amorous Licio;
All for my master's sake, Lucentio.

Re-enter GREMIO

Signior Gremio, came you from the church?
GREMIO
As willingly as e'er I came from school.
TRANIO
And is the bride and bridegroom coming home?
GREMIO
A bridegroom say you? 'tis a groom indeed,
A grumbling groom, and that the girl shall find.
TRANIO
Curster than shc? why, 'tis impossible.
GREMIO
Why he's a devil, a devil, a very fiend.
TRANIO
Why, she's a devil, a devil, the devil's dam.
GREMIO
Tut, she's a lamb, a dove, a fool to him!
I'll tell you, Sir Lucentio: when the priest

Should ask, if Katharina should be his wife,
'Ay, by gogs-wouns,' quoth he; and swore so loud,
That, all-amazed, the priest let fall the book;
And, as he stoop'd again to take it up,
The mad-brain'd bridegroom took him such a cuff
That down fell priest and book and book and priest:
'Now take them up,' quoth he, 'if any list.'

TRANIO

What said the wench when he rose again?

GREMIO

Trembled and shook; for why, he stamp'd and swore,
As if the vicar meant to cozen him.
But after many ceremonies done,
He calls for wine: 'A health!' quoth he, as if
He had been aboard, carousing to his mates
After a storm; quaff'd off the muscadel
And threw the sops all in the sexton's face;
Having no other reason
But that his beard grew thin and hungerly
And seem'd to ask him sops as he was drinking.
This done, he took the bride about the neck
And kiss'd her lips with such a clamorous smack
That at the parting all the church did echo:
And I seeing this came thence for very shame;
And after me, I know, the rout is coming.
Such a mad marriage never was before:
Hark, hark! I hear the minstrels play.

Music

*Re-enter PETRUCHIO, KATHERINA, BIANCA, BAPTISTA,
HORTENSIO, GRUMIO, and Train*

PETRUCHIO

    Gentlemen and friends, I thank you for your pains:
    I know you think to dine with me to-day,
    And have prepared great store of wedding cheer;
    But so it is, my haste doth call me hence,
    And therefore here I mean to take my leave.

BAPTISTA
    Is't possible you will away to-night?

PETRUCHIO
    I must away to-day, before night come:
    Make it no wonder; if you knew my business,
    You would entreat me rather go than stay.
    And, honest company, I thank you all,
    That have beheld me give away myself
    To this most patient, sweet and virtuous wife:
    Dine with my father, drink a health to me;
    For I must hence; and farewell to you all.

TRANIO
    Let us entreat you stay till after dinner.

PETRUCHIO
    It may not be.

GREMIO
    Let me entreat you.

PETRUCHIO
    It cannot be.

KATHERINA
    Let me entreat you.

PETRUCHIO
    I am content.

KATHERINA
    Are you content to stay?

PETRUCHIO
    I am content you shall entreat me stay;
    But yet not stay, entreat me how you can.

KATHERINA

Now, if you love me, stay.
PETRUCHIO
Grumio, my horse.
GRUMIO
Ay, sir, they be ready: the oats have eaten the horses.
KATHERINA
Nay, then,
Do what thou canst, I will not go to-day;
No, nor to-morrow, not till I please myself.
The door is open, sir; there lies your way;
You may be jogging whiles your boots are green;
For me, I'll not be gone till I please myself:
'Tis like you'll prove a jolly surly groom,
That take it on you at the first so roundly.
PETRUCHIO
O Kate, content thee; prithee, be not angry.
KATHERINA
I will be angry: what hast thou to do?
Father, be quiet; he shall stay my leisure.
GREMIO
Ay, marry, sir, now it begins to work.
KATARINA
Gentlemen, forward to the bridal dinner:
I see a woman may be made a fool,
If she had not a spirit to resist.
PETRUCHIO
They shall go forward, Kate, at thy command.
Obey the bride, you that attend on her;
Go to the feast, revel and domineer,
Carouse full measure to her maidenhead,
Be mad and merry, or go hang yourselves:
But for my bonny Kate, she must with me.
Nay, look not big, nor stamp, nor stare, nor fret;
I will be master of what is mine own:

She is my goods, my chattels; she is my house,
My household stuff, my field, my barn,
My horse, my ox, my ass, my any thing;
And here she stands, touch her whoever dare;
I'll bring mine action on the proudest he
That stops my way in Padua. Grumio,
Draw forth thy weapon, we are beset with thieves;
Rescue thy mistress, if thou be a man.
Fear not, sweet wench, they shall not touch
thee, Kate:
I'll buckler thee against a million.

Exeunt PETRUCHIO, KATHERINA, and GRUMIO

BAPTISTA
Nay, let them go, a couple of quiet ones.
GREMIO
Went they not quickly, I should die with laughing.
TRANIO
Of all mad matches never was the like.
LUCENTIO
Mistress, what's your opinion of your sister?
BIANCA
That, being mad herself, she's madly mated.
GREMIO
I warrant him, Petruchio is Kated.
BAPTISTA
Neighbours and friends, though bride and
bridegroom wants
For to supply the places at the table,
You know there wants no junkets at the feast.
Lucentio, you shall supply the bridegroom's place:
And let Bianca take her sister's room.
TRANIO
Shall sweet Bianca practise how to bride it?

BAPTISTA
    She shall, Lucentio. Come, gentlemen, let's go.

Exeunt

ACT IV

SCENE I.

PETRUCHIO'S country house.

Enter GRUMIO

GRUMIO

Fie, fie on all tired jades, on all mad masters, and
all foul ways! Was ever man so beaten? was ever
man so rayed? was ever man so weary? I am sent
before to make a fire, and they are coming after to
warm them. Now, were not I a little pot and soon
hot, my very lips might freeze to my teeth, my
tongue to the roof of my mouth, my heart in my
belly, ere I should come by a fire to thaw me: but
I, with blowing the fire, shall warm myself; for,
considering the weather, a taller man than I will
take cold. Holla, ho! Curtis.

Enter CURTIS

CURTIS

Who is that calls so coldly?

GRUMIO

A piece of ice: if thou doubt it, thou mayst slide
from my shoulder to my heel with no greater a run
but my head and my neck. A fire good Curtis.

CURTIS

Is my master and his wife coming, Grumio?

GRUMIO

O, ay, Curtis, ay: and therefore fire, fire; cast
on no water.

CURTIS

Is she so hot a shrew as she's reported?

GRUMIO

She was, good Curtis, before this frost: but, thou
knowest, winter tames man, woman and beast; for it
hath tamed my old master and my new mistress and
myself, fellow Curtis.

CURTIS

Away, you three-inch fool! I am no beast.

GRUMIO

Am I but three inches? why, thy horn is a foot; and
so long am I at the least. But wilt thou make a
fire, or shall I complain on thee to our mistress,
whose hand, she being now at hand, thou shalt soon
feel, to thy cold comfort, for being slow in thy hot
office?

CURTIS

I prithee, good Grumio, tell me, how goes the world?

GRUMIO

A cold world, Curtis, in every office but thine; and
therefore fire: do thy duty, and have thy duty; for
my master and mistress are almost frozen to death.

CURTIS

There's fire ready; and therefore, good Grumio, the
news.

GRUMIO

Why, 'Jack, boy! ho! boy!' and as much news as
will thaw.

CURTIS

Come, you are so full of cony-catching!

GRUMIO

Why, therefore fire; for I have caught extreme cold.
Where's the cook? is supper ready, the house
trimmed, rushes strewed, cobwebs swept; the
serving-men in their new fustian, their white

stockings, and every officer his wedding-garment on?
Be the jacks fair within, the jills fair without,
the carpets laid, and every thing in order?

CURTIS

All ready; and therefore, I pray thee, news.

GRUMIO

First, know, my horse is tired; my master and
mistress fallen out.

CURTIS

How?

GRUMIO

Out of their saddles into the dirt; and thereby
hangs a tale.

CURTIS

Let's ha't, good Grumio.

GRUMIO

Lend thine ear.

CURTIS

Here.

GRUMIO

There.

Strikes him

CURTIS

This is to feel a tale, not to hear a tale.

GRUMIO

And therefore 'tis called a sensible tale: and this
cuff was but to knock at your ear, and beseech
listening. Now I begin: Imprimis, we came down a
foul hill, my master riding behind my mistress,--

CURTIS

Both of one horse?

GRUMIO

What's that to thee?

CURTIS

Why, a horse.

GRUMIO

Tell thou the tale: but hadst thou not crossed me,
thou shouldst have heard how her horse fell and she
under her horse; thou shouldst have heard in how
miry a place, how she was bemoiled, how he left her
with the horse upon her, how he beat me because
her horse stumbled, how she waded through the dirt
to pluck him off me, how he swore, how she prayed,
that never prayed before, how I cried, how the
horses ran away, how her bridle was burst, how I
lost my crupper, with many things of worthy memory,
which now shall die in oblivion and thou return
unexperienced to thy grave.

CURTIS

By this reckoning he is more shrew than she.

GRUMIO

Ay; and that thou and the proudest of you all shall
find when he comes home. But what talk I of this?
Call forth Nathaniel, Joseph, Nicholas, Philip,
Walter, Sugarsop and the rest: let their heads be
sleekly combed their blue coats brushed and their
garters of an indifferent knit: let them curtsy
with their left legs and not presume to touch a hair
of my master's horse-tail till they kiss their
hands. Are they all ready?

CURTIS

They are.

GRUMIO

Call them forth.

CURTIS

Do you hear, ho? you must meet my master to
countenance my mistress.

GRUMIO
Why, she hath a face of her own.
CURTIS
Who knows not that?
GRUMIO
Thou, it seems, that calls for company to
countenance her.
CURTIS
I call them forth to credit her.
GRUMIO
Why, she comes to borrow nothing of them.

Enter four or five Serving-men

NATHANIEL
Welcome home, Grumio!
PHILIP
How now, Grumio!
JOSEPH
What, Grumio!
NICHOLAS
Fellow Grumio!
NATHANIEL
How now, old lad?
GRUMIO
Welcome, you;--how now, you;-- what, you;--fellow,
you;--and thus much for greeting. Now, my spruce
companions, is all ready, and all things neat?
NATHANIEL
All things is ready. How near is our master?
GRUMIO
E'en at hand, alighted by this; and therefore be
not--Cock's passion, silence! I hear my master.

Enter PETRUCHIO and KATHERINA

PETRUCHIO

Where be these knaves? What, no man at door
To hold my stirrup nor to take my horse!
Where is Nathaniel, Gregory, Philip?

ALL SERVING-MEN

Here, here, sir; here, sir.

PETRUCHIO

Here, sir! here, sir! here, sir! here, sir!
You logger-headed and unpolish'd grooms!
What, no attendance? no regard? no duty?
Where is the foolish knave I sent before?

GRUMIO

Here, sir; as foolish as I was before.

PETRUCHIO

You peasant swain! you whoreson malt-horse drudge!
Did I not bid thee meet me in the park,
And bring along these rascal knaves with thee?

GRUMIO

Nathaniel's coat, sir, was not fully made,
And Gabriel's pumps were all unpink'd i' the heel;
There was no link to colour Peter's hat,
And Walter's dagger was not come from sheathing:
There were none fine but Adam, Ralph, and Gregory;
The rest were ragged, old, and beggarly;
Yet, as they are, here are they come to meet you.

PETRUCHIO

Go, rascals, go, and fetch my supper in.

Exeunt Servants

Singing

Where is the life that late I led--

79

Where are those--Sit down, Kate, and welcome.--
Sound, sound, sound, sound!

Re-enter Servants with supper

Why, when, I say? Nay, good sweet Kate, be merry.
Off with my boots, you rogues! you villains, when?

Sings

It was the friar of orders grey,
As he forth walked on his way:--
Out, you rogue! you pluck my foot awry:
Take that, and mend the plucking off the other.

Strikes him

Be merry, Kate. Some water, here; what, ho!
Where's my spaniel Troilus? Sirrah, get you hence,
And bid my cousin Ferdinand come hither:
One, Kate, that you must kiss, and be acquainted with.
Where are my slippers? Shall I have some water?

Enter one with water

Come, Kate, and wash, and welcome heartily.
You whoreson villain! will you let it fall?

Strikes him

KATHERINA
    Patience, I pray you; 'twas a fault unwilling.
PETRUCHIO
    A whoreson beetle-headed, flap-ear'd knave!
    Come, Kate, sit down; I know you have a stomach.
    Will you give thanks, sweet Kate; or else shall I?
    What's this? mutton?

First Servant
  Ay.
PETRUCHIO
  Who brought it?
PETER
  I.
PETRUCHIO
  'Tis burnt; and so is all the meat.
  What dogs are these! Where is the rascal cook?
  How durst you, villains, bring it from the dresser,
  And serve it thus to me that love it not?
  Theretake it to you, trenchers, cups, and all;

Throws the meat, & c. about the stage

  You heedless joltheads and unmanner'd slaves!
  What, do you grumble? I'll be with you straight.
KATHERINA
  I pray you, husband, be not so disquiet:
  The meat was well, if you were so contented.
PETRUCHIO
  I tell thee, Kate, 'twas burnt and dried away;
  And I expressly am forbid to touch it,
  For it engenders choler, planteth anger;
  And better 'twere that both of us did fast,
  Since, of ourselves, ourselves are choleric,
  Than feed it with such over-roasted flesh.
  Be patient; to-morrow 't shall be mended,
  And, for this night, we'll fast for company:
  Come, I will bring thee to thy bridal chamber.

Exeunt

Re-enter Servants severally

NATHANIEL
  Peter, didst ever see the like?
PETER
  He kills her in her own humour.

Re-enter CURTIS

GRUMIO
  Where is he?
CURTIS
  In her chamber, making a sermon of continency to her;
  And rails, and swears, and rates, that she, poor soul,
  Knows not which way to stand, to look, to speak,
  And sits as one new-risen from a dream.
  Away, away! for he is coming hither.

Exeunt

Re-enter PETRUCHIO

PETRUCHIO
  Thus have I politicly begun my reign,
  And 'tis my hope to end successfully.
  My falcon now is sharp and passing empty;
  And till she stoop she must not be full-gorged,
  For then she never looks upon her lure.
  Another way I have to man my haggard,
  To make her come and know her keeper's call,
  That is, to watch her, as we watch these kites
  That bate and beat and will not be obedient.
  She eat no meat to-day, nor none shall eat;
  Last night she slept not, nor to-night she shall not;
  As with the meat, some undeserved fault
  I'll find about the making of the bed;
  And here I'll fling the pillow, there the bolster,

This way the coverlet, another way the sheets:
Ay, and amid this hurly I intend
That all is done in reverend care of her;
And in conclusion she shall watch all night:
And if she chance to nod I'll rail and brawl
And with the clamour keep her still awake.
This is a way to kill a wife with kindness;
And thus I'll curb her mad and headstrong humour.
He that knows better how to tame a shrew,
Now let him speak: 'tis charity to show.

Exit

SCENE II.

Padua. Before BAPTISTA'S house.

Enter TRANIO and HORTENSIO

TRANIO

    Is't possible, friend Licio, that Mistress Bianca
    Doth fancy any other but Lucentio?
    I tell you, sir, she bears me fair in hand.

HORTENSIO

    Sir, to satisfy you in what I have said,
    Stand by and mark the manner of his teaching.

Enter BIANCA and LUCENTIO

LUCENTIO

    Now, mistress, profit you in what you read?

BIANCA

    What, master, read you? first resolve me that.

LUCENTIO

    I read that I profess, the Art to Love.

BIANCA

And may you prove, sir, master of your art!
LUCENTIO
   While you, sweet dear, prove mistress of my heart!
HORTENSIO
   Quick proceeders, marry! Now, tell me, I pray,
   You that durst swear at your mistress Bianca
   Loved none in the world so well as Lucentio.
TRANIO
   O despiteful love! unconstant womankind!
   I tell thee, Licio, this is wonderful.
HORTENSIO
   Mistake no more: I am not Licio,
   Nor a musician, as I seem to be;
   But one that scorn to live in this disguise,
   For such a one as leaves a gentleman,
   And makes a god of such a cullion:
   Know, sir, that I am call'd Hortensio.
TRANIO
   Signior Hortensio, I have often heard
   Of your entire affection to Bianca;
   And since mine eyes are witness of her lightness,
   I will with you, if you be so contented,
   Forswear Bianca and her love for ever.
HORTENSIO
   See, how they kiss and court! Signior Lucentio,
   Here is my hand, and here I firmly vow
   Never to woo her no more, but do forswear her,
   As one unworthy all the former favours
   That I have fondly flatter'd her withal.
TRANIO
   And here I take the unfeigned oath,
   Never to marry with her though she would entreat:
   Fie on her! see, how beastly she doth court him!
HORTENSIO

Would all the world but he had quite forsworn!
For me, that I may surely keep mine oath,
I will be married to a wealthy widow,
Ere three days pass, which hath as long loved me
As I have loved this proud disdainful haggard.
And so farewell, Signior Lucentio.
Kindness in women, not their beauteous looks,
Shall win my love: and so I take my leave,
In resolution as I swore before.

Exit

TRANIO
Mistress Bianca, bless you with such grace
As 'longeth to a lover's blessed case!
Nay, I have ta'en you napping, gentle love,
And have forsworn you with Hortensio.
BIANCA
Tranio, you jest: but have you both forsworn me?
TRANIO
Mistress, we have.
LUCENTIO
Then we are rid of Licio.
TRANIO
I' faith, he'll have a lusty widow now,
That shall be wood and wedded in a day.
BIANCA
God give him joy!
TRANIO
Ay, and he'll tame her.
BIANCA
He says so, Tranio.
TRANIO
Faith, he is gone unto the taming-school.
BIANCA

The taming-school! what, is there such a place?
TRANIO
    Ay, mistress, and Petruchio is the master;
    That teacheth tricks eleven and twenty long,
    To tame a shrew and charm her chattering tongue.

Enter BIONDELLO

BIONDELLO
    O master, master, I have watch'd so long
    That I am dog-weary: but at last I spied
    An ancient angel coming down the hill,
    Will serve the turn.
TRANIO
    What is he, Biondello?
BIONDELLO
    Master, a mercatante, or a pedant,
    I know not what; but format in apparel,
    In gait and countenance surely like a father.
LUCENTIO
    And what of him, Tranio?
TRANIO
    If he be credulous and trust my tale,
    I'll make him glad to seem Vincentio,
    And give assurance to Baptista Minola,
    As if he were the right Vincentio
    Take in your love, and then let me alone.

Exeunt LUCENTIO and BIANCA

Enter a Pedant

Pedant
    God save you, sir!
TRANIO

And you, sir! you are welcome.
Travel you far on, or are you at the farthest?
Pedant
Sir, at the farthest for a week or two:
But then up farther, and as for as Rome;
And so to Tripoli, if God lend me life.
TRANIO
What countryman, I pray?
Pedant
Of Mantua.
TRANIO
Of Mantua, sir? marry, God forbid!
And come to Padua, careless of your life?
Pedant
My life, sir! how, I pray? for that goes hard.
TRANIO
'Tis death for any one in Mantua
To come to Padua. Know you not the cause?
Your ships are stay'd at Venice, and the duke,
For private quarrel 'twixt your duke and him,
Hath publish'd and proclaim'd it openly:
'Tis, marvel, but that you are but newly come,
You might have heard it else proclaim'd about.
Pedant
Alas! sir, it is worse for me than so;
For I have bills for money by exchange
From Florence and must here deliver them.
TRANIO
Well, sir, to do you courtesy,
This will I do, and this I will advise you:
First, tell me, have you ever been at Pisa?
Pedant
Ay, sir, in Pisa have I often been,
Pisa renowned for grave citizens.

TRANIO
   Among them know you one Vincentio?
Pedant
   I know him not, but I have heard of him;
   A merchant of incomparable wealth.
TRANIO
   He is my father, sir; and, sooth to say,
   In countenance somewhat doth resemble you.
BIONDELLO
   [Aside] As much as an apple doth an oyster,
   and all one.
TRANIO
   To save your life in this extremity,
   This favour will I do you for his sake;
   And think it not the worst of an your fortunes
   That you are like to Sir Vincentio.
   His name and credit shall you undertake,
   And in my house you shall be friendly lodged:
   Look that you take upon you as you should;
   You understand me, sir: so shall you stay
   Till you have done your business in the city:
   If this be courtesy, sir, accept of it.
Pedant
   O sir, I do; and will repute you ever
   The patron of my life and liberty.
TRANIO
   Then go with me to make the matter good.
   This, by the way, I let you understand;
   my father is here look'd for every day,
   To pass assurance of a dower in marriage
   'Twixt me and one Baptista's daughter here:
   In all these circumstances I'll instruct you:
   Go with me to clothe you as becomes you.

                    Exeunt

                       88

SCENE III.

A room in PETRUCHIO'S house.

Enter KATHERINA and GRUMIO

GRUMIO

No, no, forsooth; I dare not for my life.

KATHERINA

The more my wrong, the more his spite appears:

What, did he marry me to famish me?

Beggars, that come unto my father's door,

Upon entreaty have a present aims;

If not, elsewhere they meet with charity:

But I, who never knew how to entreat,

Nor never needed that I should entreat,

Am starved for meat, giddy for lack of sleep,

With oath kept waking and with brawling fed:

And that which spites me more than all these wants,

He does it under name of perfect love;

As who should say, if I should sleep or eat,

'Twere deadly sickness or else present death.

I prithee go and get me some repast;

I care not what, so it be wholesome food.

GRUMIO

What say you to a neat's foot?

KATHERINA

'Tis passing good: I prithee let me have it.

GRUMIO

I fear it is too choleric a meat.

How say you to a fat tripe finely broil'd?

KATHERINA

I like it well: good Grumio, fetch it me.

GRUMIO

I cannot tell; I fear 'tis choleric.
What say you to a piece of beef and mustard?
KATHERINA
A dish that I do love to feed upon.
GRUMIO
Ay, but the mustard is too hot a little.
KATHERINA
Why then, the beef, and let the mustard rest.
GRUMIO
Nay then, I will not: you shall have the mustard,
Or else you get no beef of Grumio.
KATHERINA
Then both, or one, or any thing thou wilt.
GRUMIO
Why then, the mustard without the beef.
KATHERINA
Go, get thee gone, thou false deluding slave,

Beats him

That feed'st me with the very name of meat:
Sorrow on thee and all the pack of you,
That triumph thus upon my misery!
Go, get thee gone, I say.

Enter PETRUCHIO and HORTENSIO with meat

PETRUCHIO
How fares my Kate? What, sweeting, all amort?
HORTENSIO
Mistress, what cheer?
KATHERINA
Faith, as cold as can be.
PETRUCHIO
Pluck up thy spirits; look cheerfully upon me.

Here love; thou see'st how diligent I am
To dress thy meat myself and bring it thee:
I am sure, sweet Kate, this kindness merits thanks.
What, not a word? Nay, then thou lovest it not;
And all my pains is sorted to no proof.
Here, take away this dish.
KATHERINA
I pray you, let it stand.
PETRUCHIO
The poorest service is repaid with thanks;
And so shall mine, before you touch the meat.
KATHERINA
I thank you, sir.
HORTENSIO
Signior Petruchio, fie! you are to blame.
Come, mistress Kate, I'll bear you company.
PETRUCHIO
[Aside] Eat it up all, Hortensio, if thou lovest me.
Much good do it unto thy gentle heart!
Kate, eat apace: and now, my honey love,
Will we return unto thy father's house
And revel it as bravely as the best,
With silken coats and caps and golden rings,
With ruffs and cuffs and fardingales and things;
With scarfs and fans and double change of bravery,
With amber bracelets, beads and all this knavery.
What, hast thou dined? The tailor stays thy leisure,
To deck thy body with his ruffling treasure.

Enter Tailor

Come, tailor, let us see these ornaments;
Lay forth the gown.

Enter Haberdasher

What news with you, sir?
Haberdasher
Here is the cap your worship did bespeak.
PETRUCHIO
Why, this was moulded on a porringer;
A velvet dish: fie, fie! 'tis lewd and filthy:
Why, 'tis a cockle or a walnut-shell,
A knack, a toy, a trick, a baby's cap:
Away with it! come, let me have a bigger.
KATHERINA
I'll have no bigger: this doth fit the time,
And gentlewomen wear such caps as these
PETRUCHIO
When you are gentle, you shall have one too,
And not till then.
HORTENSIO
[Aside] That will not be in haste.
KATHERINA
Why, sir, I trust I may have leave to speak;
And speak I will; I am no child, no babe:
Your betters have endured me say my mind,
And if you cannot, best you stop your ears.
My tongue will tell the anger of my heart,
Or else my heart concealing it will break,
And rather than it shall, I will be free
Even to the uttermost, as I please, in words.
PETRUCHIO
Why, thou say'st true; it is a paltry cap,
A custard-coffin, a bauble, a silken pie:
I love thee well, in that thou likest it not.
KATHERINA
Love me or love me not, I like the cap;
And it I will have, or I will have none.

Exit Haberdasher

PETRUCHIO

Thy gown? why, ay: come, tailor, let us see't.

O mercy, God! what masquing stuff is here?

What's this? a sleeve? 'tis like a demi-cannon:

What, up and down, carved like an apple-tart?

Here's snip and nip and cut and slish and slash,

Like to a censer in a barber's shop:

Why, what, i' devil's name, tailor, call'st thou this?

HORTENSIO

[Aside] I see she's like to have neither cap nor gown.

Tailor

You bid me make it orderly and well,

According to the fashion and the time.

PETRUCHIO

Marry, and did; but if you be remember'd,

I did not bid you mar it to the time.

Go, hop me over every kennel home,

For you shall hop without my custom, sir:

I'll none of it: hence! make your best of it.

KATHERINA

I never saw a better-fashion'd gown,

More quaint, more pleasing, nor more commendable:

Belike you mean to make a puppet of me.

PETRUCHIO

Why, true; he means to make a puppet of thee.

Tailor

She says your worship means to make

a puppet of her.

PETRUCHIO

O monstrous arrogance! Thou liest, thou thread,
thou thimble,

Thou yard, three-quarters, half-yard, quarter, nail!

93

Thou flea, thou nit, thou winter-cricket thou!
Braved in mine own house with a skein of thread?
Away, thou rag, thou quantity, thou remnant;
Or I shall so be-mete thee with thy yard
As thou shalt think on prating whilst thou livest!
I tell thee, I, that thou hast marr'd her gown.

Tailor

Your worship is deceived; the gown is made
Just as my master had direction:
Grumio gave order how it should be done.

GRUMIO

I gave him no order; I gave him the stuff.

Tailor

But how did you desire it should be made?

GRUMIO

Marry, sir, with needle and thread.

Tailor

But did you not request to have it cut?

GRUMIO

Thou hast faced many things.

Tailor

I have.

GRUMIO

Face not me: thou hast braved many men; brave not
me; I will neither be faced nor braved. I say unto
thee, I bid thy master cut out the gown; but I did
not bid him cut it to pieces: ergo, thou liest.

Tailor

Why, here is the note of the fashion to testify

PETRUCHIO

Read it.

GRUMIO

The note lies in's throat, if he say I said so.

Tailor

[Reads] 'Imprimis, a loose-bodied gown:'

GRUMIO

Master, if ever I said loose-bodied gown, sew me in
the skirts of it, and beat me to death with a bottom
of brown thread: I said a gown.

PETRUCHIO

Proceed.

Tailor

[Reads] 'With a small compassed cape:'

GRUMIO

I confess the cape.

Tailor

[Reads] 'With a trunk sleeve:'

GRUMIO

I confess two sleeves.

Tailor

[Reads] 'The sleeves curiously cut.'

PETRUCHIO

Ay, there's the villany.

GRUMIO

Error i' the bill, sir; error i' the bill.
I commanded the sleeves should be cut out and
sewed up again; and that I'll prove upon thee,
though thy little finger be armed in a thimble.

Tailor

This is true that I say: an I had thee
in place where, thou shouldst know it.

GRUMIO

I am for thee straight: take thou the
bill, give me thy mete-yard, and spare not me.

HORTENSIO

God-a-mercy, Grumio! then he shall have no odds.

PETRUCHIO

Well, sir, in brief, the gown is not for me.

GRUMIO
  You are i' the right, sir: 'tis for my mistress.
PETRUCHIO
  Go, take it up unto thy master's use.
GRUMIO
  Villain, not for thy life: take up my mistress'
  gown for thy master's use!
PETRUCHIO
  Why, sir, what's your conceit in that?
GRUMIO
  O, sir, the conceit is deeper than you think for:
  Take up my mistress' gown to his master's use!
  O, fie, fie, fie!
PETRUCHIO
  [Aside] Hortensio, say thou wilt see the tailor paid.
  Go take it hence; be gone, and say no more.
HORTENSIO
  Tailor, I'll pay thee for thy gown tomorrow:
  Take no unkindness of his hasty words:
  Away! I say; commend me to thy master.

Exit Tailor

PETRUCHIO
  Well, come, my Kate; we will unto your father's
  Even in these honest mean habiliments:
  Our purses shall be proud, our garments poor;
  For 'tis the mind that makes the body rich;
  And as the sun breaks through the darkest clouds,
  So honour peereth in the meanest habit.
  What is the jay more precious than the lark,
  Because his fathers are more beautiful?
  Or is the adder better than the eel,
  Because his painted skin contents the eye?
  O, no, good Kate; neither art thou the worse

For this poor furniture and mean array.
if thou account'st it shame. lay it on me;
And therefore frolic: we will hence forthwith,
To feast and sport us at thy father's house.
Go, call my men, and let us straight to him;
And bring our horses unto Long-lane end;
There will we mount, and thither walk on foot
Let's see; I think 'tis now some seven o'clock,
And well we may come there by dinner-time.

KATHERINA
I dare assure you, sir, 'tis almost two;
And 'twill be supper-time ere you come there.

PETRUCHIO
It shall be seven ere I go to horse:
Look, what I speak, or do, or think to do,
You are still crossing it. Sirs, let't alone:
I will not go to-day; and ere I do,
It shall be what o'clock I say it is.

HORTENSIO
[Aside] Why, so this gallant will command the sun.

Exeunt

SCENE IV.

Padua. Before BAPTISTA'S house.

Enter TRANIO, and the Pedant dressed like VINCENTIO

TRANIO
Sir, this is the house: please it you that I call?
Pedant
Ay, what else? and but I be deceived
Signior Baptista may remember me,
Near twenty years ago, in Genoa,
Where we were lodgers at the Pegasus.

TRANIO
'Tis well; and hold your own, in any case,
With such austerity as 'longeth to a father.
Pedant
I warrant you.

Enter BIONDELLO

But, sir, here comes your boy;
'Twere good he were school'd.
TRANIO
Fear you not him. Sirrah Biondello,
Now do your duty throughly, I advise you:
Imagine 'twere the right Vincentio.
BIONDELLO
Tut, fear not me.
TRANIO
But hast thou done thy errand to Baptista?
BIONDELLO
I told him that your father was at Venice,
And that you look'd for him this day in Padua.
TRANIO
Thou'rt a tall fellow: hold thee that to drink.
Here comes Baptista: set your countenance, sir.

Enter BAPTISTA and LUCENTIO

Signior Baptista, you are happily met.

To the Pedant

Sir, this is the gentleman I told you of:
I pray you stand good father to me now,
Give me Bianca for my patrimony.
Pedant
Soft son!

98

Sir, by your leave: having come to Padua
To gather in some debts, my son Lucentio
Made me acquainted with a weighty cause
Of love between your daughter and himself:
And, for the good report I hear of you
And for the love he beareth to your daughter
And she to him, to stay him not too long,
I am content, in a good father's care,
To have him match'd; and if you please to like
No worse than I, upon some agreement
Me shall you find ready and willing
With one consent to have her so bestow'd;
For curious I cannot be with you,
Signior Baptista, of whom I hear so well.

BAPTISTA

Sir, pardon me in what I have to say:
Your plainness and your shortness please me well.
Right true it is, your son Lucentio here
Doth love my daughter and she loveth him,
Or both dissemble deeply their affections:
And therefore, if you say no more than this,
That like a father you will deal with him
And pass my daughter a sufficient dower,
The match is made, and all is done:
Your son shall have my daughter with consent.

TRANIO

I thank you, sir. Where then do you know best
We be affied and such assurance ta'en
As shall with either part's agreement stand?

BAPTISTA

Not in my house, Lucentio; for, you know,
Pitchers have ears, and I have many servants:
Besides, old Gremio is hearkening still;
And happily we might be interrupted.

TRANIO

Then at my lodging, an it like you:
There doth my father lie; and there, this night,
We'll pass the business privately and well.
Send for your daughter by your servant here:
My boy shall fetch the scrivener presently.
The worst is this, that, at so slender warning,
You are like to have a thin and slender pittance.

BAPTISTA

It likes me well. Biondello, hie you home,
And bid Bianca make her ready straight;
And, if you will, tell what hath happened,
Lucentio's father is arrived in Padua,
And how she's like to be Lucentio's wife.

BIONDELLO

I pray the gods she may with all my heart!

TRANIO

Dally not with the gods, but get thee gone.

Exit BIONDELLO

Signior Baptista, shall I lead the way?
Welcome! one mess is like to be your cheer:
Come, sir; we will better it in Pisa.

BAPTISTA

I follow you.

Exeunt TRANIO, Pedant, and BAPTISTA

Re-enter BIONDELLO

BIONDELLO

Cambio!

LUCENTIO

What sayest thou, Biondello?

BIONDELLO
You saw my master wink and laugh upon you?
LUCENTIO
Biondello, what of that?
BIONDELLO
Faith, nothing; but has left me here behind, to
expound the meaning or moral of his signs and tokens.
LUCENTIO
I pray thee, moralize them.
BIONDELLO
Then thus. Baptista is safe, talking with the
deceiving father of a deceitful son.
LUCENTIO
And what of him?
BIONDELLO
His daughter is to be brought by you to the supper.
LUCENTIO
And then?
BIONDELLO
The old priest of Saint Luke's church is at your
command at all hours.
LUCENTIO
And what of all this?
BIONDELLO
I cannot tell; expect they are busied about a
counterfeit assurance: take you assurance of her,
'cum privilegio ad imprimendum solum:' to the
church; take the priest, clerk, and some sufficient
honest witnesses: If this be not that you look for,
I have no more to say, But bid Bianca farewell for
ever and a day.
LUCENTIO
Hearest thou, Biondello?
BIONDELLO

I cannot tarry: I knew a wench married in an
afternoon as she went to the garden for parsley to
stuff a rabbit; and so may you, sir: and so, adieu,
sir. My master hath appointed me to go to Saint
Luke's, to bid the priest be ready to come against
you come with your appendix.

Exit

LUCENTIO
I may, and will, if she be so contented:
She will be pleased; then wherefore should I doubt?
Hap what hap may, I'll roundly go about her:
It shall go hard if Cambio go without her.

Exit

SCENE V.

A public road.

*Enter PETRUCHIO, KATHERINA, HORTENSIO, and
Servants*

PETRUCHIO
Come on, i' God's name; once more toward our father's.
Good Lord, how bright and goodly shines the moon!
KATHERINA
The moon! the sun: it is not moonlight now.
PETRUCHIO
I say it is the moon that shines so bright.
KATHERINA
I know it is the sun that shines so bright.
PETRUCHIO
Now, by my mother's son, and that's myself,
It shall be moon, or star, or what I list,
Or ere I journey to your father's house.

Go on, and fetch our horses back again.
Evermore cross'd and cross'd; nothing but cross'd!
HORTENSIO
Say as he says, or we shall never go.
KATHERINA
Forward, I pray, since we have come so far,
And be it moon, or sun, or what you please:
An if you please to call it a rush-candle,
Henceforth I vow it shall be so for me.
PETRUCHIO
I say it is the moon.
KATHERINA
I know it is the moon.
PETRUCHIO
Nay, then you lie: it is the blessed sun.
KATHERINA
Then, God be bless'd, it is the blessed sun:
But sun it is not, when you say it is not;
And the moon changes even as your mind.
What you will have it named, even that it is;
And so it shall be so for Katharina.
HORTENSIO
Petruchio, go thy ways; the field is won.
PETRUCHIO
Well, forward, forward! thus the bowl should run,
And not unluckily against the bias.
But, soft! company is coming here.

Enter VINCENTIO

To VINCENTIO

Good morrow, gentle mistress: where away?
Tell me, sweet Kate, and tell me truly too,

Hast thou beheld a fresher gentlewoman?
Such war of white and red within her cheeks!
What stars do spangle heaven with such beauty,
As those two eyes become that heavenly face?
Fair lovely maid, once more good day to thee.
Sweet Kate, embrace her for her beauty's sake.

HORTENSIO
A' will make the man mad, to make a woman of him.

KATHERINA
Young budding virgin, fair and fresh and sweet,
Whither away, or where is thy abode?
Happy the parents of so fair a child;
Happier the man, whom favourable stars
Allot thee for his lovely bed-fellow!

PETRUCHIO
Why, how now, Kate! I hope thou art not mad:
This is a man, old, wrinkled, faded, wither'd,
And not a maiden, as thou say'st he is.

KATHERINA
Pardon, old father, my mistaking eyes,
That have been so bedazzled with the sun
That everything I look on seemeth green:
Now I perceive thou art a reverend father;
Pardon, I pray thee, for my mad mistaking.

PETRUCHIO
Do, good old grandsire; and withal make known
Which way thou travellest: if along with us,
We shall be joyful of thy company.

VINCENTIO
Fair sir, and you my merry mistress,
That with your strange encounter much amazed me,
My name is call'd Vincentio; my dwelling Pisa;
And bound I am to Padua; there to visit
A son of mine, which long I have not seen.

PETRUCHIO
What is his name?
VINCENTIO
Lucentio, gentle sir.
PETRUCHIO
Happily we met; the happier for thy son.
And now by law, as well as reverend age,
I may entitle thee my loving father:
The sister to my wife, this gentlewoman,
Thy son by this hath married. Wonder not,
Nor be grieved: she is of good esteem,
Her dowery wealthy, and of worthy birth;
Beside, so qualified as may beseem
The spouse of any noble gentleman.
Let me embrace with old Vincentio,
And wander we to see thy honest son,
Who will of thy arrival be full joyous.
VINCENTIO
But is it true? or else is it your pleasure,
Like pleasant travellers, to break a jest
Upon the company you overtake?
HORTENSIO
I do assure thee, father, so it is.
PETRUCHIO
Come, go along, and see the truth hereof;
For our first merriment hath made thee jealous.

Exeunt all but HORTENSIO

HORTENSIO
Well, Petruchio, this has put me in heart.
Have to my widow! and if she be froward,
Then hast thou taught Hortensio to be untoward.

Exit

105

ACT V

SCENE I.

Padua. Before LUCENTIO'S house.

GREMIO discovered. Enter behind BIONDELLO, LUCENTIO, and BIANCA

BIONDELLO
Softly and swiftly, sir; for the priest is ready.
LUCENTIO
I fly, Biondello: but they may chance to need thee
at home; therefore leave us.
BIONDELLO
Nay, faith, I'll see the church o' your back; and
then come back to my master's as soon as I can.

Exeunt LUCENTIO, BIANCA, and BIONDELLO

GREMIO
I marvel Cambio comes not all this while.

Enter PETRUCHIO, KATHERINA, VINCENTIO, GRUMIO, with Attendants

PETRUCHIO
Sir, here's the door, this is Lucentio's house:
My father's bears more toward the market-place;
Thither must I, and here I leave you, sir.
VINCENTIO
You shall not choose but drink before you go:
I think I shall command your welcome here,
And, by all likelihood, some cheer is toward.

Knocks

GREMIO

They're busy within; you were best knock louder.

Pedant looks out of the window

Pedant

What's he that knocks as he would beat down the gate?

VINCENTIO

Is Signior Lucentio within, sir?

Pedant

He's within, sir, but not to be spoken withal.

VINCENTIO

What if a man bring him a hundred pound or two, to
make merry withal?

Pedant

Keep your hundred pounds to yourself: he shall
need none, so long as I live.

PETRUCHIO

Nay, I told you your son was well beloved in Padua.
Do you hear, sir? To leave frivolous circumstances,
I pray you, tell Signior Lucentio that his father is
come from Pisa, and is here at the door to speak with
him.

Pedant

Thou liest: his father is come from Padua and here
looking out at the window.

VINCENTIO

Art thou his father?

Pedant

Ay, sir; so his mother says, if I may believe her.

PETRUCHIO

[To VINCENTIO] Why, how now, gentleman! why, this
is flat knavery, to take upon you another man's name.

Pedant

Lay hands on the villain: I believe a' means to

cozen somebody in this city under my countenance.

Re-enter BIONDELLO

BIONDELLO
I have seen them in the church together: God send
'em good shipping! But who is here? mine old
master Vincentio! now we are undone and brought to
nothing.
VINCENTIO
[Seeing BIONDELLO]
Come hither, crack-hemp.
BIONDELLO
Hope I may choose, sir.
VINCENTIO
Come hither, you rogue. What, have you forgot me?
BIONDELLO
Forgot you! no, sir: I could not forget you, for I
never saw you before in all my life.
VINCENTIO
What, you notorious villain, didst thou never see
thy master's father, Vincentio?
BIONDELLO
What, my old worshipful old master? yes, marry, sir:
see where he looks out of the window.
VINCENTIO
Is't so, indeed.

Beats BIONDELLO

BIONDELLO
Help, help, help! here's a madman will murder me.

Exit

Pedant

Help, son! help, Signior Baptista!

Exit from above

PETRUCHIO
Prithee, Kate, let's stand aside and see the end of
this controversy.

They retire

Re-enter Pedant below; TRANIO, BAPTISTA, and Servants

TRANIO
Sir, what are you that offer to beat my servant?
VINCENTIO
What am I, sir! nay, what are you, sir? O immortal
gods! O fine villain! A silken doublet! a velvet
hose! a scarlet cloak! and a copatain hat! O, I
am undone! I am undone! while I play the good
husband at home, my son and my servant spend all at
the university.
TRANIO
How now! what's the matter?
BAPTISTA
What, is the man lunatic?
TRANIO
Sir, you seem a sober ancient gentleman by your
habit, but your words show you a madman. Why, sir,
what 'cerns it you if I wear pearl and gold? I
thank my good father, I am able to maintain it.
VINCENTIO
Thy father! O villain! he is a sailmaker in Bergamo.
BAPTISTA
You mistake, sir, you mistake, sir. Pray, what do
you think is his name?

VINCENTIO

His name! as if I knew not his name: I have brought
him up ever since he was three years old, and his
name is Tranio.

Pedant

Away, away, mad ass! his name is Lucentio and he is
mine only son, and heir to the lands of me, Signior
Vincentio.

VINCENTIO

Lucentio! O, he hath murdered his master! Lay hold
on him, I charge you, in the duke's name. O, my
son, my son! Tell me, thou villain, where is my son
Lucentio?

TRANIO

Call forth an officer.

Enter one with an Officer

Carry this mad knave to the gaol. Father Baptista,
I charge you see that he be forthcoming.

VINCENTIO

Carry me to the gaol!

GREMIO

Stay, officer: he shall not go to prison.

BAPTISTA

Talk not, Signior Gremio: I say he shall go to prison.

GREMIO

Take heed, Signior Baptista, lest you be
cony-catched in this business: I dare swear this
is the right Vincentio.

Pedant

Swear, if thou darest.

GREMIO

Nay, I dare not swear it.

TRANIO

Then thou wert best say that I am not Lucentio.

GREMIO

Yes, I know thee to be Signior Lucentio.

BAPTISTA

Away with the dotard! to the gaol with him!

VINCENTIO

Thus strangers may be hailed and abused: O
monstrous villain!

Re-enter BIONDELLO, with LUCENTIO and BIANCA

BIONDELLO

O! we are spoiled and--yonder he is: deny him,
forswear him, or else we are all undone.

LUCENTIO

[Kneeling] Pardon, sweet father.

VINCENTIO

Lives my sweet son?

*Exeunt BIONDELLO, TRANIO, and Pedant, as fast as may
be*

BIANCA

Pardon, dear father.

BAPTISTA

How hast thou offended?
Where is Lucentio?

LUCENTIO

Here's Lucentio,
Right son to the right Vincentio;
That have by marriage made thy daughter mine,
While counterfeit supposes bleared thine eyne.

GREMIO

Here's packing, with a witness to deceive us all!

VINCENTIO

Where is that damned villain Tranio,
That faced and braved me in this matter so?
BAPTISTA
Why, tell me, is not this my Cambio?
BIANCA
Cambio is changed into Lucentio.
LUCENTIO
Love wrought these miracles. Bianca's love
Made me exchange my state with Tranio,
While he did bear my countenance in the town;
And happily I have arrived at the last
Unto the wished haven of my bliss.
What Tranio did, myself enforced him to;
Then pardon him, sweet father, for my sake.
VINCENTIO
I'll slit the villain's nose, that would have sent
me to the gaol.
BAPTISTA
But do you hear, sir? have you married my daughter
without asking my good will?
VINCENTIO
Fear not, Baptista; we will content you, go to: but
I will in, to be revenged for this villany.

Exit

BAPTISTA
And I, to sound the depth of this knavery.

Exit

LUCENTIO
Look not pale, Bianca; thy father will not frown.

Exeunt LUCENTIO and BIANCA

GREMIO

My cake is dough; but I'll in among the rest,
Out of hope of all, but my share of the feast.

Exit

KATHERINA

Husband, let's follow, to see the end of this ado.

PETRUCHIO

First kiss me, Kate, and we will.

KATHERINA

What, in the midst of the street?

PETRUCHIO

What, art thou ashamed of me?

KATHERINA

No, sir, God forbid; but ashamed to kiss.

PETRUCHIO

Why, then let's home again. Come, sirrah, let's away.

KATHERINA

Nay, I will give thee a kiss: now pray thee, love, stay.

PETRUCHIO

Is not this well? Come, my sweet Kate:
Better once than never, for never too late.

Exeunt

SCENE II.

Padua. LUCENTIO'S house.

*Enter BAPTISTA, VINCENTIO, GREMIO, the Pedant,
LUCENTIO, BIANCA, PETRUCHIO, KATHERINA,
HORTENSIO, and Widow, TRANIO, BIONDELLO, and
GRUMIO the Serving-men with Tranio bringing in a
banquet*

LUCENTIO

At last, though long, our jarring notes agree:
And time it is, when raging war is done,
To smile at scapes and perils overblown.
My fair Bianca, bid my father welcome,
While I with self-same kindness welcome thine.
Brother Petruchio, sister Katharina,
And thou, Hortensio, with thy loving widow,
Feast with the best, and welcome to my house:
My banquet is to close our stomachs up,
After our great good cheer. Pray you, sit down;
For now we sit to chat as well as eat.

PETRUCHIO

Nothing but sit and sit, and eat and eat!

BAPTISTA

Padua affords this kindness, son Petruchio.

PETRUCHIO

Padua affords nothing but what is kind.

HORTENSIO

For both our sakes, I would that word were true.

PETRUCHIO

Now, for my life, Hortensio fears his widow.

Widow

Then never trust me, if I be afeard.

PETRUCHIO

You are very sensible, and yet you miss my sense:
I mean, Hortensio is afeard of you.

Widow

He that is giddy thinks the world turns round.

PETRUCHIO

Roundly replied.

KATHERINA

Mistress, how mean you that?

Widow

Thus I conceive by him.

PETRUCHIO
Conceives by me! How likes Hortensio that?
HORTENSIO
My widow says, thus she conceives her tale.
PETRUCHIO
Very well mended. Kiss him for that, good widow.
KATHERINA
'He that is giddy thinks the world turns round:'
I pray you, tell me what you meant by that.
Widow
Your husband, being troubled with a shrew,
Measures my husband's sorrow by his woe:
And now you know my meaning,
KATHERINA
A very mean meaning.
Widow
Right, I mean you.
KATHERINA
And I am mean indeed, respecting you.
PETRUCHIO
To her, Kate!
HORTENSIO
To her, widow!
PETRUCHIO
A hundred marks, my Kate does put her down.
HORTENSIO
That's my office.
PETRUCHIO
Spoke like an officer; ha' to thee, lad!

Drinks to HORTENSIO

BAPTISTA
How likes Gremio these quick-witted folks?
GREMIO

Believe me, sir, they butt together well.
BIANCA
    Head, and butt! an hasty-witted body
    Would say your head and butt were head and horn.
VINCENTIO
    Ay, mistress bride, hath that awaken'd you?
BIANCA
    Ay, but not frighted me; therefore I'll sleep again.
PETRUCHIO
    Nay, that you shall not: since you have begun,
    Have at you for a bitter jest or two!
BIANCA
    Am I your bird? I mean to shift my bush;
    And then pursue me as you draw your bow.
    You are welcome all.

Exeunt BIANCA, KATHERINA, and Widow

PETRUCHIO
    She hath prevented me. Here, Signior Tranio.
    This bird you aim'd at, though you hit her not;
    Therefore a health to all that shot and miss'd.
TRANIO
    O, sir, Lucentio slipp'd me like his greyhound,
    Which runs himself and catches for his master.
PETRUCHIO
    A good swift simile, but something currish.
TRANIO
    'Tis well, sir, that you hunted for yourself:
    'Tis thought your deer does hold you at a bay.
BAPTISTA
    O ho, Petruchio! Tranio hits you now.
LUCENTIO
    I thank thee for that gird, good Tranio.
HORTENSIO

Confess, confess, hath he not hit you here?

PETRUCHIO

A' has a little gall'd me, I confess;

And, as the jest did glance away from me,

'Tis ten to one it maim'd you two outright.

BAPTISTA

Now, in good sadness, son Petruchio,

I think thou hast the veriest shrew of all.

PETRUCHIO

Well, I say no: and therefore for assurance

Let's each one send unto his wife;

And he whose wife is most obedient

To come at first when he doth send for her,

Shall win the wager which we will propose.

HORTENSIO

Content. What is the wager?

LUCENTIO

Twenty crowns.

PETRUCHIO

Twenty crowns!

I'll venture so much of my hawk or hound,

But twenty times so much upon my wife.

LUCENTIO

A hundred then.

HORTENSIO

Content.

PETRUCHIO

A match! 'tis done.

HORTENSIO

Who shall begin?

LUCENTIO

That will I.

Go, Biondello, bid your mistress come to me.

BIONDELLO

I go.

Exit

BAPTISTA
  Son, I'll be your half, Bianca comes.
LUCENTIO
  I'll have no halves; I'll bear it all myself.

Re-enter BIONDELLO

How now! what news?
BIONDELLO
  Sir, my mistress sends you word
  That she is busy and she cannot come.
PETRUCHIO
  How! she is busy and she cannot come!
  Is that an answer?
GREMIO
  Ay, and a kind one too:
  Pray God, sir, your wife send you not a worse.
PETRUCHIO
  I hope better.
HORTENSIO
  Sirrah Biondello, go and entreat my wife
  To come to me forthwith.

Exit BIONDELLO

PETRUCHIO
  O, ho! entreat her!
  Nay, then she must needs come.
HORTENSIO
  I am afraid, sir,
  Do what you can, yours will not be entreated.

Re-enter BIONDELLO

Now, where's my wife?
BIONDELLO
She says you have some goodly jest in hand:
She will not come: she bids you come to her.
PETRUCHIO
Worse and worse; she will not come! O vile,
Intolerable, not to be endured!
Sirrah Grumio, go to your mistress;
Say, I command her to come to me.

Exit GRUMIO

HORTENSIO
I know her answer.
PETRUCHIO
What?
HORTENSIO
She will not.
PETRUCHIO
The fouler fortune mine, and there an end.
BAPTISTA
Now, by my holidame, here comes Katharina!

Re-enter KATHERINA

KATHERINA
What is your will, sir, that you send for me?
PETRUCHIO
Where is your sister, and Hortensio's wife?
KATHERINA
They sit conferring by the parlor fire.
PETRUCHIO
Go fetch them hither: if they deny to come.
Swinge me them soundly forth unto their husbands:

Away, I say, and bring them hither straight.

Exit KATHERINA

LUCENTIO
Here is a wonder, if you talk of a wonder.
HORTENSIO
And so it is: I wonder what it bodes.
PETRUCHIO
Marry, peace it bodes, and love and quiet life,
And awful rule and right supremacy;
And, to be short, what not, that's sweet and happy?
BAPTISTA
Now, fair befal thee, good Petruchio!
The wager thou hast won; and I will add
Unto their losses twenty thousand crowns;
Another dowry to another daughter,
For she is changed, as she had never been.
PETRUCHIO
Nay, I will win my wager better yet
And show more sign of her obedience,
Her new-built virtue and obedience.
See where she comes and brings your froward wives
As prisoners to her womanly persuasion.

Re-enter KATHERINA, with BIANCA and Widow

Katharina, that cap of yours becomes you not:
Off with that bauble, throw it under-foot.
Widow
Lord, let me never have a cause to sigh,
Till I be brought to such a silly pass!
BIANCA
Fie! what a foolish duty call you this?
LUCENTIO

I would your duty were as foolish too:
The wisdom of your duty, fair Bianca,
Hath cost me an hundred crowns since supper-time.
BIANCA
The more fool you, for laying on my duty.
PETRUCHIO
Katharina, I charge thee, tell these headstrong women
What duty they do owe their lords and husbands.
Widow
Come, come, you're mocking: we will have no telling.
PETRUCHIO
Come on, I say; and first begin with her.
Widow
She shall not.
PETRUCHIO
I say she shall: and first begin with her.
KATHERINA
Fie, fie! unknit that threatening unkind brow,
And dart not scornful glances from those eyes,
To wound thy lord, thy king, thy governor:
It blots thy beauty as frosts do bite the meads,
Confounds thy fame as whirlwinds shake fair buds,
And in no sense is meet or amiable.
A woman moved is like a fountain troubled,
Muddy, ill-seeming, thick, bereft of beauty;
And while it is so, none so dry or thirsty
Will deign to sip or touch one drop of it.
Thy husband is thy lord, thy life, thy keeper,
Thy head, thy sovereign; one that cares for thee,
And for thy maintenance commits his body
To painful labour both by sea and land,
To watch the night in storms, the day in cold,
Whilst thou liest warm at home, secure and safe;
And craves no other tribute at thy hands

But love, fair looks and true obedience;
Too little payment for so great a debt.
Such duty as the subject owes the prince
Even such a woman oweth to her husband;
And when she is froward, peevish, sullen, sour,
And not obedient to his honest will,
What is she but a foul contending rebel
And graceless traitor to her loving lord?
I am ashamed that women are so simple
To offer war where they should kneel for peace;
Or seek for rule, supremacy and sway,
When they are bound to serve, love and obey.
Why are our bodies soft and weak and smooth,
Unapt to toil and trouble in the world,
But that our soft conditions and our hearts
Should well agree with our external parts?
Come, come, you froward and unable worms!
My mind hath been as big as one of yours,
My heart as great, my reason haply more,
To bandy word for word and frown for frown;
But now I see our lances are but straws,
Our strength as weak, our weakness past compare,
That seeming to be most which we indeed least are.
Then vail your stomachs, for it is no boot,
And place your hands below your husband's foot:
In token of which duty, if he please,
My hand is ready; may it do him ease.

PETRUCHIO

Why, there's a wench! Come on, and kiss me, Kate.

LUCENTIO

Well, go thy ways, old lad; for thou shalt ha't.

VINCENTIO

'Tis a good hearing when children are toward.

LUCENTIO

But a harsh hearing when women are froward.

PETRUCHIO

Come, Kate, we'll to bed.

We three are married, but you two are sped.

To LUCENTIO

'Twas I won the wager, though you hit the white;

And, being a winner, God give you good night!

Exeunt PETRUCHIO and KATHERINA

HORTENSIO

Now, go thy ways; thou hast tamed a curst shrew.

LUCENTIO

'Tis a wonder, by your leave, she will be tamed so.

Exeunt

Biography

A Short Life of Edward de Vere,
17th Earl of Oxford

by Dr. Kevin Gilvary, President
The de Vere Society

He was born on 12 April 1550 at Castle Hedingham, his family's ancestral home. His father, John de Vere, 16th Earl, was Lord Great Chamberlain and attended the coronations of both Mary and Elizabeth Tudor. His mother was Margaret Golding. Edward was 11 when, in 1561, Queen Elizabeth visited Hedingham for four days of masques, feasting and entertainments. When his father died in 1562, young Oxford left to become, like Bertram in *All's Well that Ends Well*, a ward of the Crown under the guardianship of William Cecil, the Queen's private secretary (later Lord Burghley, Lord Treasurer). His mother married Charles Tyrrell and seems to have passed out of the boy's life. His sister Mary went to live with her stepfather and the siblings were not reunited for some years.

According to a curriculum in Cecil's own hand, Edward de Vere's daily studies included dancing, French, Latin, writing and drawing, cosmography, penmanship, riding, shooting, exercise and prayer. Edward de Vere showed a prodigious talent for scholarship from his early years, and we may ascribe his lifelong love of learning to the influence of two of his early tutors. The first was Sir Thomas Smith who was, perhaps, England's most respected Greek scholar and the former Cambridge tutor of Sir William Cecil. It was, no doubt, through Cecil's influence that Edward de Vere spent some time living in the household of Smith in his early years, during which time he spent about five months at Smith's alma mater, Queens' College, Cambridge. Smith was a scholar of widely varied interests – this was reflected in his 400-volume library, some of which is still extant at Cambridge. De Vere's other tutor was Laurence Nowell, who was not only an accomplished cartographer but was also England's premier scholar of Anglo-Saxon literature – it was Nowell who possessed the only known copy of *Beowulf*.

Another important influence on Edward de Vere's early studies was his maternal uncle Arthur Golding, an officer in the Court of Wards under Cecil, who is credited with the translation of Ovid's *Metamorphoses*, published in 1567, a book widely recognised as having a major influence on 'Shakespeare'.

Following on from his matriculation at Cambridge in November 1558, Edward was awarded an honorary MA by Cambridge during a Royal progress in August 1564, and another degree by Oxford University during a Royal progress in 1566. Edward de Vere then attended Gray's Inn to study law. One notable feature of the Elizabethan Inns of Court was a tradition of mounting dramatic productions and of hosting the various touring companies of players.

In 1570 he served in a military campaign in Scotland under the Earl of Sussex. By 1571, he was reported as a leading luminary of the Court and, for a time, a favourite of Queen Elizabeth. In December 1571 he married Anne Cecil, aged 15, daughter of his guardian. This was a dynastic marriage where all the advantage accrued to Cecil who, ennobled as Baron Burghley, had reduced the social gap between himself and the young Earl.

While Oxford was away on a Grand Tour of Europe, he heard that his daughter Elizabeth Vere had been born in July 1575. On his return in early 1576, he appeared to have been convinced that Elizabeth was not his child; consequently he became estranged from Anne for five years, and exiled himself from Court, taking up residence in the Savoy and concerning himself with literary and musical patronage.

Already, in 1573, *Cardanus Comfort* (the Consolations of Boethius) had been translated from Latin by Thomas Bedingfield and dedicated to Oxford; and published with a preface written by him. In 1576 an anthology, *A Paradise of Daintie Devices*, including several poems by Oxford, was published. These are juvenile works but already show affinities, in both style and thought, with those of the mature Shakespeare.

Oxford's Grand Tour had taken in Paris, Strasbourg, Venice, Genoa, Florence, Palermo and, on his way back through France, Rousillon – the setting for *Love's Labour's Lost*. Oxford spent the best part of a year travelling in Italy in 1576, and becoming involved with moneylenders. He came back to England fluent in Italian and well acquainted with the northern Italian cities, to be satirised by Gabriel Harvey as 'The Italian Earl'. On his way back his ship was attacked by pirates in the English Channel (cf. *Hamlet*). Fourteen of 'Shakespeare's' plays have Italian settings, in which he put his detailed knowledge of the country, beyond pure book knowledge, to good use.

1573 saw the birth of Henry Wriothesley, Earl of Southampton. Although history has not bequeathed to us any evidence of a direct relationship between the two men, in the relatively small world of the royal Court, they must have been acquainted with each other. The poems *Venus and Adonis* (1593) and *The Rape of Lucrece* (1594) were dedicated to Southampton. These were the first works to be published under the name 'Shakespeare' and for the next five years the records show the byline 'Shakespeare' to have been associated exclusively with these two poems. Plays under the name 'Shakespeare' did not appear in print until 1598, the year that Lord Burghley died.

In May 1577 Oxford invested in Frobisher's voyage in the ship *Edward Bonaventure*. Despite its name, the ship's voyage across the Atlantic in search of the North-West Passage lost money; consequently he was forced to sell three estates (cf. Hamlet's words 'I am but mad north-north-west' II.1.). In 1578 he invested in Frobisher's second expedition, which also lost money, forcing further sales of estates.

He was mentioned by Gabriel Harvey in an address to Queen Elizabeth in July 1578, as a prolific private poet and one 'whose countenance shakes spears'. In the same year John Lyly, Oxford's secretary, published *Euphues.The Anatomy of Wit*, followed in 1579 by *Euphues and his England*, dedicated to Oxford. These two books launched the fashion for 'Euphuism', a style characterized by high-flown language, satirized in *Love's Labour's Lost*.

In March 1581 Oxford's mistress, Anne Vavasour, who was one of Queen Elizabeth's Ladies of the Bedchamber, gave birth to a son. The lovers and their son were sent to the Tower by an infuriated Queen but swiftly released (cf. *Measure for Measure*). After his release, Oxford was wounded in a street-fight provoked by Thomas Knyvet, a kinsman of Anne Vavasour; affrays continued in the streets of London between the rival gangs of supporters for over a year (cf.*Romeo and Juliet*).

In December 1581 he resumed living with his long-suffering and devoted wife, and accepted Elizabeth

Vere as his child. Tragically, their only son died one day after his birth. Three more daughters followed, of whom Susan and Bridget survived.

In 1584, Robert Greene's *Gwydonius; the Card of Fancy* was dedicated to him, identifying him as a 'pre-eminent writer'. In 1586, when he was 36, he served on the tribunal which condemned Mary, Queen of Scots to execution.

In the same year, the Queen awarded Oxford an unconditional pension of £1,000 a year for life (about £500,000 at today's value). The motive for this uncharacteristic generosity on the part of the Queen remains a mystery – no accounting was required of Oxford. Her successor, King James I, continued to pay the pension. In reply to Sir Robert Cecil's request that Lord Sheffield's pension be increased, the King refused, saying, 'Great Oxford got no more . . .', leaving us to wonder why Great Oxford? His greatness does not seem to have resided in war or any of the known offices of State. Perhaps a clue can be found in a letter to Burghley, written in 1594, in which Edward de Vere seeks his favour in a matter involving what he describes as 'in mine office' and that this office is beholden to the Queen.

In 1589, George Puttenham published *The Arte of English Poesie* and this contains the most telling recognition of Edward de Vere's literary standing amongst his contemporaries: 'And in her Majesties time that now is are sprong up an other crew of Courtly makers Noble men and Gentlemen of her Majesties owne servantes, who have written excellently well as it would appeare if their doings could be found out and made publicke with the rest, of which number is first that noble Gentleman Edward Earle of Oxford.'

In 1588 his wife Anne, daughter of Lord Burghley, died and in extant letters written at this time, it is reported that Burghley is so incapacitated by grief over the death of his favourite daughter that he is incapable of conducting any Privy Council business.

Three years later, in 1591, Oxford married another of the Queen's Maids of Honour, Elizabeth Trentham, with whom he finally became the father of a male heir; Henry de Vere, 18th Earl of Oxford. Although there is evidence of his continued involvement in Court affairs, from the date of this marriage Edward de Vere's life at his new home at King's Place in Hackney is perhaps the most obscure of his entire life.

In 1594, his ship the *Edward Bonaventure* was wrecked in Bermuda (cf. *The Tempest*). In January 1595, Elizabeth Vere married William Stanley, 6th Earl of Derby, another literary earl who maintained his own company of players – many scholars believe that *A Midsummer Night's Dream* was written for these festivities which were attended by the whole royal Court.

On September 7 1598, Francis Meres' *Palladis Tamia* was registered for publication, naming Oxford as the 'best for comedy'. This is a vital document in Shakespearean history because it includes the first mention of 'Shakespeare' as a playwright, attributing twelve plays to him; until then Shakespeare's reputation had rested on the two narrative poems only.

Oxford suffered all his life from financial difficulties, much of which can be traced to the fact that Queen Elizabeth handed out the bulk of his estate to her favourite courtier the Earl of Leicester during Oxford's minority as a royal ward (estates which Oxford found almost impossible to reclaim), and the ruinous debt she placed upon him over his marriage to Anne Cecil. It is, however, notable that his new brother-in-law, the wealthy Staffordshire landowner and Knight of the Shire Francis Trentham, took over the management of Edward de

Vere's near-bankrupt estate from 1591 and gradually nursed it back to health so that, when Oxford died, all of his massive debts had been cleared.

On the Queen's death in 1603 Oxford wrote eloquently to Sir Robert Cecil, son and heir of Lord Burghley, of his 'great grief'. He wrote, 'In this common shipwreck, mine is above all the rest, who least regarded, though often comforted, she hath left to try my fortune among the alterations of time and chance'.

Oxford died in Hackney in 1604, cause unknown. Parish records state that he was buried in Hackney Church on July 6, but a family history by his first cousin Percival Golding, states 'Edward de Veer ... a man in mind and body absolutely accomplished with honorable endowments ... lieth buried at Westminster'. No record of such a burial can now be traced in Westminster Abbey, where there is a Vere family tomb.

The Aftermath of Oxford's life and death

During the winter season 1604-05, six of Shakespeare's plays were presented at Court by command of King James I. This has an air of commemoration. In 1609 the *Sonnets* were published in a pirated edition. The famous dedication describes the author as 'our ever-living', a phrase invariably used only of the dead.

In 1622 Henry Peacham published, in *The Compleat Gentelman*, a list of poets who made Elizabeth's reign a 'golden age'. Unaccountably, he omitted Shakespeare but placed the Earl of Oxford in first place in his list – perhaps he knew them to be the same person. This is unlike Meres who included them both – maybe one reason was because he didn't know Oxford and Shakespeare were the same person.

We do not know who instigated publication of the First Folio Edition of the Shakespeare plays in 1623, but there is no mention of any executor or relative of Shakspere of Stratford in connection with it. However, of the two brothers who financed it and to whom it was dedicated, one – Philip Earl of Montgomery – was the husband of Oxford's daughter Susan, while the other – William Earl of Pembroke – had once been a suitor for her sister Bridget. Pembroke was Lord Chamberlain, the supreme authority in the world of theatre, and thus in a position to decide which plays were to be published and which suppressed. We also know that Ben Jonson, who wrote much of the introductory material, was an intimate associate of the de Vere family after Oxford's death. The First Folio was therefore very much a family affair, but the family was not the one in Stratford-on-Avon.

An AfterVerse

For those with yet an interest
In strenuous debate
We've compiled a list of books and films
Your appetite to sate.
From this study clear your mind
Of doubt and all misgiving-
Who from us has long since gone
And who is ever-living.

Selected References & Bibliography
About the Author
Edward de Vere, 17th Earl of Oxford

Books

♦ Anderson, M. (2005). *Shakespeare by Another Name: The Life of Edward de Vere, Earl of Oxford, The Man who was Shakespeare.* New York: Gotham Books. *--A physicist by training with research interest in how evidence supports or negates a theory, Mark Anderson spent ten years investigating Edward de Vere as the author of Shake-speare's works.*

♦Farina, William. (2006). *De Vere as Shakespeare: An Oxfordian Reading of the Canon.* Jefferson, NC. McFarland & Company.

--Each of the plays and poems is individually assessed and explored in its own chapter, using the innumerable connections between the text itself and the life of its author, Edward de Vere.

♦ Looney, J. Thomas (2018). *Shakespeare Identified.* Cary, N.C. Veritas Publicaations.
--First published in 1920 this book began the modern Oxfordian movement. From reading it, Sigmund Freud became convinced and John Galsworthy called it "the best detective story I ever read."

♦ Ogburn, C. (1992). *The Mysterious William Shakespeare.* McLean (Va.): EPM.
--An in depth exploration and must read foundational book on the authorship question.

♦Sobran, Joseph. (1997). *Alias Shakespeare: Solving the Greatest Literary Mystery of All Time.* New York; The Free Press, A Division of Simon & Schuster.
--A concise exploration of the puzzling questions surrounding the authorship controversy with the evidence decisively supporting the case for Edward de Vere, the 17th Earl of Oxford, as the rightful author of the Shakespeare plays and poems.

♦Whittemore, Hank. (2016), *100 Reasons Shake-speare Was the Earl of Oxford.* Somerville MA. Forever Press.
►Also with further discussion and public comment at: *Hank Whittemore's Shakespeare Blog.*
https://hankwhittemore.com/
--In both the book and online blog cited above, Whittemore presents a concise introduction to the

authorship question that examines 100 different aspects, from biographical and historical records, that point to Edward de Vere as the true writer of the Shake-speare plays and poems.

Websites & Videos

► De Vere Society. (2019). The de Vere Society – Dedicated to the proposition that the works of Shakespeare were written by Edward de Vere, 17th Earl of Oxford. [online] Deveresociety.co.uk. Available at: https://deveresociety.co.uk
--A very complete resource with substantial biographical and authorship information and links.

► The Oxford Fellowship (2019). Shakespeare Oxford Fellowship | Research and Discussion of the Shakespeare Authorship Question. [online] Shakespeare Oxford Fellowship. Available at: https://shakespeareoxfordfellowship.org/
--A seminal online resource especially focusing on the authorship question.

► Waugh, A. (2019). Alexander Waugh. [online] YouTube. Available at: https://www.youtube.com/channel/UCHN7SCKlsa9lPYJ mqqQ2uIg/featured/
OR simply search: 'Alexander Waugh'
--Alexander Waugh is a leading authorship scholar who has produced many fascinating video presentations on the authorship question. This link is to his YouTube Channel.

► Columbia Pictures & Centropolis Entertainment. (2011). *Anonymous.* Produced and directed by Roland Emmerich. [DVD]
--*This mainstream film is both entertaining and enlightening. It presents a superb dramatization of the character of Edward de Vere, setting out in detail the historical and personal context which made his anonymous authorship necessary.*

►Centropolis Entertainment and First Folio Pictures. *Last Will and Testament.* (2012). [DVD]
--*A thoughtful and ground-breaking video documentary introduction to the Shakespeare authorship question.*

Acknowledgment
Our sincere thanks to
The de Vere Society
and
The Shakespeare Oxford Fellowship
*for their inspiration, help and support
in creating this series.*

Attributions
*--Character list from Wikipedia under
the Creative Commons License 3.0
--Play text from the Moby(tm) editions
in the public domain*

Photos
Coat of Arms of Edward de Vere
Source: Wikimedia.org
Author: George Baker / Public domain

The Keep at Castle Hedingham
Source: geograph.org.uk
Author: David Phillips / CC BY-SA 2.0

The de Vere Family Coat of Arms
Source: Wikimedia
Author: Rs-nourse / CC BY-SA 3.0
(https://creativecommons.org/licenses/by-sa/3.0)

View from The Minstrels' Gallery, Hedingham Castle
Source: geograph.org.uk/p/3162585
Photo by: © PAUL FARMER - cc-by-sa/2.0

Cover/Inside: The Welbeck portrait of Edward de Vere (1575).
Artist unknown. National Portrait Gallery, London.

This work has been edited and produced by

Verus Publishing
www.verusbooks.com

V | P